WALKING

WITH THE

WISE

for Health and Vitality

Compiled By

Linda Forsythe

&

Brad J. King, M.S., MFS

MENTORS Publishing House, Inc.
San Diego, California

www.mentorsmagazine.com

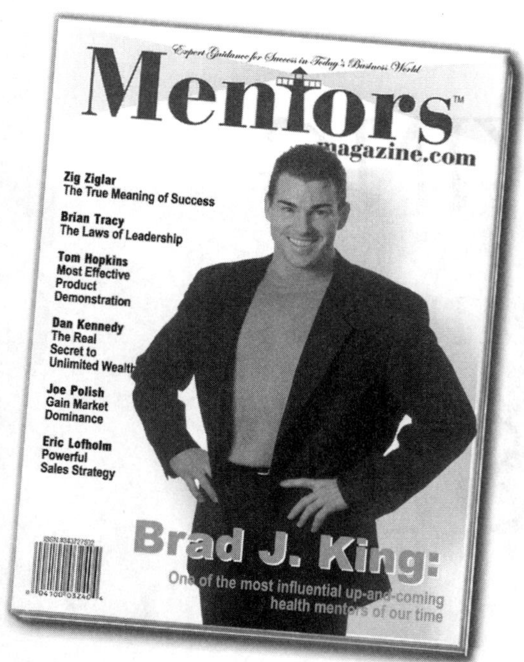

Need Inspiration, Information or Mentoring?

Register Now For FREE Membership

Visit our Web site!
www.mentorsmagazine.com

- **FREE** newsletters filled with guidance, from our nationally recognized mentors

- **FREE** online subscription to MENTORS magazine

- **FREE TELESEMINARS** by experts who coach you toward success in business and life

- Talk to our Mentors **LIVE every Monday** such as:
    - Anthony Robbins
    - Zig Ziglar
    - Brian Tracy
    - Brad King
    - Tom Hopkins
    - Deepak Chopra

www.mentorsmagazine.com

www.mentorsmagazine.com

When Health is absent...

Wisdom cannot reveal itself

Art cannot become manifest

Strength cannot be exerted

Wealth is useless and

Reason is powerless.

– Herophiles, 300 B.C.

WALKING WITH THE WISE™ for Health and Vitality

ISBN 0-9729875-1-7

Printed in the United States of America

9 8 7 6 5 4 3 2 1 – 10

Published by MENTORS Publishing House, Inc.
10755-F Scripps Poway Pkwy. #530
San Diego, CA 92131
Telephone: (858) 277-9700
Web: www.mentorsmagazine.com

This book is available at quantity discounts for bulk purchases and for branding by businesses and organizations. For further information, or to learn more about MENTORS Magazine™, mentorsmagazine.com™, Walking with the Wise™ *and other products and services of MENTORS Publishing House, Inc., contact: (858) 277-9700.*

Cover Design, page composition, typography & illustration by Kim Muslusky, KimCo. Graphics, Poway, CA. Cover photo and MENTORS logo retouching by Sam Defais. Cover photo by Karl Andy Anderson/ImageState.

The publisher would like to acknowledge the many publishers and individuals who granted us permission to reprint their cited material or have written specifically for this book.

Foreword

Become Who
You Were Born to Be!

By Brad J. King, M.S., MFS

How many times in your life do you get the opportunity to bring together a group of individuals who have greatly impacted the lives of thousands – even millions – of people around the world? How many times do you get the opportunity to collaborate on a project with the greatest minds in the health sciences? How many times can you disseminate information to the world that may change people's lives for the better? There can never be enough times in anyone's life to have these opportunities – which is exactly why I jumped at the chance to bring this book together!

I am a nutritional researcher who never seems to have enough time in the day to get everything done. When MENTORS magazine asked me if I would be interested in compiling an anthology with 30 of the world's top health professionals, I knew the project would take more time than I had. Still, it took all of a few seconds to respond with a resounding ABSOLUTELY!

I would be hand-picking Health Mentors I knew would be able to provide a health-changing paradigm shift in peoples' lives. My prerequisite for each contributor was that in one way or another they would have changed numerous individuals' lives for the better. Each Health Mentor would be asked to provide a chapter on a topic of interest that he/she felt should be brought to the public's attention. And once this life-altering information was available, you (the reader) would assume the responsibility of what you wanted to do with the newfound knowledge.

How do you define health? *Webster's* dictionary defines it as: "The condition of being sound in body, mind, or spirit; *especially* freedom from physical disease or pain." How many of you right now can honestly say you are sound in body, mind and spirit? How many of you can say that you are 100% free from physical disease or pain? The fact is, at some point in our lives – no matter how sound we may feel – we will experience some degree of physical illness or pain, even if it is in the form of a simple cold or a twisted ankle.

We are all human and therefore subject to the reality that we are only as strong as our bodies are able to hold up against the onslaughts of every day life. Let's face it, the five or so pounds of skin that cover our muscles, skeleton, organs and blood is not exactly made of armor. As human beings, we are completely vulnerable to our environment, not to mention our dietary and life-style choices.

We are in a very real sense a collage of nearly 100 trillion cells that are bathed in the very essence of what we place in our mouths, our minds and our souls every second of every day. We may be able to feel the heartbeat that pulses nearly 100 thousand times each day, delivering the vital nutrients and oxygen through the nearly 60 thousand miles of piping to each and every one of our cells while carting away each cell's garbage for disposal. The question is, can we actually feel the way each and every one of these cells reacts to our everyday choices?

The truth is, we take for granted – at least the majority of the time – that our heart will beat everyday, supplying every inch of us with the vital oxygen and nutrients we need to sustain our lives. We don't think about it, it just happens. But make no bones about it, every single time you place a morsel of food into your mouth, every single time you exercise or lie on a couch, every single time you stress over events that may or may not happen, deep within your body's tiniest structures, millions of biochemical reactions are taking place. These biochemical reactions receive their cues from commands given out by your genes, which in turn receive their instructions from every single thing you do in a 24-hour cycle.

You may indeed never feel each one of your cells working desperately to provide you with abundant health and vitality, but you will eventually feel the outcome of every one of your choices. The donut and coffee breakfast followed by the fast food lunch and the microwave dinner coupled with the stressed out day, the false light of television (that you believe helps you relax) and the lack of proper sleep – that never quite replenishes your body's needs, may go on for years before it manifests itself as a malfunction somewhere in your body. But the fact remains that every single choice you have made contributed to your body's inability to stay healthy.

In this day and age we make too many excuses for the things we know we shouldn't do. Your health depends upon the only person that can make a difference – You! There is no excuse to smoke, be lazy, and not get sufficient exercise. And there is certainly no excuse to constantly place processed foods in your mouth and expect your body to perform at peak efficiency.

I love life! Therefore, the vast majority of the time, I am careful with how I promote the health of my body, mind and soul. But that doesn't make me a saint when it comes to my health, so how can I expect anyone else to be? The majority of the time, I eat high quality foods, exercise, get enough quality sleep and do my best to be positive. But every once and a while I'll let loose and eat some of my favorite foods (trust me, they're not the best choices) or have a few glasses of my favorite red wine. The point is, I can do it guilt-free because the majority of the time I am conscious of my everyday choices and their effects upon my health. The question is, are you conscious of the choices you make each and every day?

If you are someone who lives by the adage: "You only live once," then ask yourself, "How long do I want to remain alive?" Life is not just about living—simply existing—it's about being alive while we are here on this earth. Life is definitely a miracle, but feeling alive is a constant work in progress. Oscar Wilde said it best: "To live is the rarest thing in the world. Most people exist, that is all."

The truth is that the majority of our society accepts their less than optimal health status as the way they are supposed to feel with each advancing year. They accept this as the truth, when in fact it is far from it. Within us, we hold the key to life. We can loosen the chains of ill health and become truly alive or we can keep tightening them – the choice is up to us.

It is never too early, or too late, for that matter, to change your habits for the better. Your past does not have to equal your future. If you learn to alter your negative patterns for healthier positive ones, you can change the course of your destiny. The experts that have come together in this anthology are here to help you chart your new course.

Once you acknowledge the obstacles keeping you from living life to its fullest potential and apply the newfound skills you will learn in the following pages, a healthy vibrant life is yours for the taking. Motivation may get you started, but habit will keep you going.

Start the process of change today – the quality of your life literally depends upon it! As Elrond the Elf King said to Aragorn in the *Return of the King:* **"Become who you were born to be!"**

Brad J. King, M.S., MFS, is a well-respected nutritional researcher, performance nutritionist, fitness expert and Canadian Sports Nutrition Hall of Fame inductee. He is also the scientific director of the Fat Loss Research Institute. Brad has developed numerous gold medal-winning nutritional products for the health industry and has appeared as a leading health expert on hundreds of radio and television shows, including the Today Show. He is the author of the international bestseller *Fat Wars: 45 Days to Transform Your Body, Fat Wars Action Planner, Bio-Age: 10 Steps to a Younger You,* and the newly released *7 Steps to Awaken Your Body: The Fat Wars Un-Diet Plan.*

For more information on winning the Fat Wars and to sign up for a monthly Fat Wars Chronicle see: www.fatwars.com.

Table of Contents

LAST WORDS FROM USUALLY SILENT OBSERVERS...

Acknowledgments

And Many Thanks...

Brad King - For my partner in the creation of this book. Thank you for finding the majority of the health professionals (including yourself), who have contributed and offered invaluable advice. You have made a positive difference in the lives of many.

Lena Osborn - For my savvy French business partner who has provided both heart and brains to this company. Congratulations on your United States citizenship and thank you for coming here from France. Your business management, networking, legal and financial planning genius has helped MENTORS magazine spread its wings as a world wide conglomerate.

Kim Muslusky - For being an incredible art director and graphic designer. It is because of you that all of our magazines and books are completed in record time and the finished products have a great look.

Cheri Hoffman - For being the Editor-In-Chief of the century!!! Thank you for working with every article contributor (a huge task in itself). Thank you for making sure that what was written by each contributor was worthy to be printed in a book with high standards. It takes talent and patience to edit well known health professionals and physicians!

Tiffany Young - For being my executive assistant and the MENTORS teleseminar program director. Thank you for keeping everything in line and running smoothly. Your organizational and public relations skills are phenomenal! You are an asset to all of us at MENTORS International.

MENTORS magazine webmasters: Russell Speck, Tom Tenover, Paul Schweinfurter – For making MENTORS magazine THE leader in the industry by creating, engineering and maintaining MENTORS on the Internet. (www.mentorsmagazine.com) All of you have worked together as a "well oiled machine" to create our multi-million dollar site and bring mentoring information to the world.

Sam Defais - For doing an outstanding job to touch up the cover photo and revising the MENTORS magazine mast-head. You show great promise as a graphic designer.

Our article contributors - For taking the time from your very busy schedules to provide words of wisdom that will change the lives of all who read them. You are all health angels!!!

With Love and Gratitude,

Linda Forsythe

It is Time to Love Ourselves

(We're Worth It!!!)

By Linda Forsythe

One of the many benefits of being the Publisher of MENTORS magazine and the *Walking With the Wise* book series is that it is my job to read every single article that will be sent to press for all of our publications. To carefully read the words of wisdom from some of the top mentors in the world has had a profound effect on my life and in changing the way I think. Every day I receive a multitude of e-mails and letters from individuals around the globe who have received the same positive benefits as I have. I have found that when we choose to listen and apply good advice, our lives start to evolve toward abundance. (Notice I used the word, "APPLY!")

If we would listen to good advice from people who mentor us toward a happier lifestyle, then we would be well on our way down the right path. Unfortunately, that happier lifestyle doesn't seem to "happen" for many people. Why is that? We have found that people don't always apply what they've learned. This one particular component of "application of good knowledge" is what is taught in our publications over and over again. Why are we such strong advocates of this? Because when we don't apply what we've learned, nothing changes and therefore we begin to whine about our fate. Yes...it becomes whining when we continue to complain. When we KNOW what to do to fix something and then don't do it!

Unfortunately nobody knows this better than I. When I personally don't want to do something that will mean a major change in my life, I procrastinate and rationalize. I am extremely good at coming up with excuses. It's only human. Allow me to give you a rather uncomfortable case in point...

It is now the day of New Year's Eve and I'm finally sitting down to write this Publisher's Note. (To the enormous relief of my staff!!!) I have been whining about taking the time to get this article done because I've been SOOOOOO busy. This delayed action isn't necessarily a bad thing except we are dangerously close to going to press. I had to ask myself, "Why am I procrastinating on this when I normally adhere strictly to deadlines and my article was due weeks ago?" The answer came when I sat down to write my New Year's resolutions yesterday. (Notice how I chose to do that before this article?) ***Writing this note for a book on health was going to force me to look at myself in the health arena.*** As a mentor, it is important that you know how to live the type of life that you teach about. Hence my problem. You see...I have been a very bad girl these past two years when it came to living a healthy lifestyle. What makes it worse is I have absolutely NO EXCUSE. Especially since I was a nurse in the Cardiac Care Unit for 15 years. I know what I need to do for the most part, but haven't been *applying* the knowledge. The only answer for this lack of application in my case is I haven't loved myself enough.

In all fairness...we do need to change one bad habit at a time and I've had a LOT of bad habits to change. The business that I've started with MENTORS magazine has changed my life for the better each time we've put out a publication. Reading these articles all the time has allowed me to become aware of what I need to change within myself. Sometimes painfully aware. One thing that has been noticed by those around me is that I have seriously changed for the better from the way I was 10 years ago. This is only because I've made a sincere dedicated effort to change. (I guess this makes me a poster girl for what can happen if you listen to mentors!) Some of us will change a bad habit only because the repercussions will outweigh the uncomfortable process of the change. Well, that's me! Crisis seems to be the only thing that moves me out of my comfort zone – even if that comfort zone isn't so comfortable. I'm afraid I'm also rather stubborn.

When I look back on my days of working in the Cardiac Intensive Care Unit of multiple hospitals (I was a travel nurse), I would see the same type of cardiac cases consistently. A large majority of patients wouldn't have been there if they had lived a different lifestyle. Many had moved through their lives with a sense of complacency. The harsh repercussions of their lifestyle choices came crashing down on them, many times without warning. Quite a few had the mindset of, "It will never happen to me." Part of this sense of complacency is exacerbated by the fact that our heart beats automatically without our thinking about it. The Autonomic Nervous System will pump our heart and squeeze life-giving blood with all of its nutrients, oxygen, bacterial fighting and balancing chemicals to the rest of our body. If the body doesn't receive healthy and oxygenated blood in any area of the body, for any reason, life begins to go wrong. It can also be a subtle accumulation of problems that happen over time. The body of an elder person will tell an accurate story of how riotous a life was lived in the younger years.

The various or combined *choices* of bad diet, lack of exercise, out-of-control stress, drug and/or alcohol abuse, negative thinking and lack of love causes the heart to stop functioning correctly. A very subtle but vital thing is happening to us without our awareness and it is easy to take it for granted. (Until it breaks down.)

The patients I took care of survived a heart attack or were hospitalized for procedures because of the state of their heart. After this serious "wake up" call...most chose to make a dramatic and positive change to their lifestyle. All of a sudden the thought of changing their diet, adding more exercise, reducing stress and stopping bad habits became a priority for them. In fact, in most cases the decision was instantaneous.

After enduring the very scary ordeal of a painful heart attack, or surgery, a patient would then move on to Cardiac Rehab. This would involve them having to walk a few feet at a time with a therapist, while they were hooked up to an oxygen tank, Oxymeter, IV and cardiac monitor. Walking just a few feet is a major ordeal for these people at first. The patient is literally starting from scratch. Most move on eventually to a healthier lifestyle than when they were first admitted into the CCU. It took a very uncomfortable crisis to knock them out of their state of complacency. Those who chose not to make positive changes and remained in denial were generally seen back in the CCU – if they lived through another attack.

One of the vital lessons we have taught with our previous books and magazines is the importance of health. All the money, family and abundance in the world means very little when you don't have your health. In fact most people who have worked hard all of their lives to build up riches while ignoring their health have then spent those riches in order to get their health back.

Why does it seem to be a choice for some people to ignore something as vital and necessary as a healthy body in our search for a life of abundance and prosperity? As I mentioned earlier, it's because we either don't love ourselves enough or we just don't really fathom what could happen until we lose it.

My excuse for ignoring myself was that I was so busy building a business and attending to the needs of my family. My health has been failing because of it, although I'm still not in that extreme state of crisis...YET. I also know I'm not far from it. Since I've stopped watching my diet, stopped exercising and have been immersed in a very high state of stress for the last two years, my body is definitely showing the signs of this lack of attention by manifesting problems.

I also know what will happen if I continue on this present path. I saw it happen to others for many years so I personally don't have a lack of awareness. How about you? Are you aware of what could happen if you continue to ignore your health? Force yourself right this second to think about it even though you are tempted to move on (or do what I did and come up with excuses to procrastinate). It is literally vital that you take the time and come to a decision on what to do next.

Now *I* need to "walk my own talk." Reading the articles in this book and writing this note has helped me to remember what I need to do. I saw my doctor last week and know that sensible exercise is okay for me to start. I had gone to him in the first place because I haven't been feeling well. Now I need to love myself enough to *apply my knowledge.*

I'm off to hand in this article to our editor and then out the door to take a vigorous walk while breathing in the clean ocean air of sunny San Diego. No... I won't over-do it because I want to stick with it. I'll just start small and build to good health. Changing my diet and the way I deal with stress is also going to be part of this New Year's Resolution. I even wrote down a plan with a schedule. I also have our readers who are going to hold me accountable to this promise, so now I'm absolutely committed! (YIKES...no wonder I've been procrastinating!!!)

Just the mere thought of really living life and experiencing this beautiful world around me has already lifted a load of stress off of my shoulders. Why would I want to continue to procrastinate? Why would you? The prosperity mind set of good health is a choice. I hope you choose to walk on this path with me.

Linda Forsythe is the Founder/Publisher of MENTORS magazine and CEO of MENTORS International. She has dedicated herself to helping others lead a life of true abundance and prosperity. Her desire to learn, combined with excellent networking skills, and a passion for empowering others has led her to create magazines, books, teleseminars, conferences, workshops and Web sites. She also has appeared in print, television, radio and electronic media. She would love to hear from you via e-mail at Linda@mentorsmagazine.com.

30 Mentors

for
Vitality & Good Health

© 2004 Kim Muslusky

Thoughts:
A Fountain of Health & Well Being

By Alejandra Armas

Good health is not only the lack of disease and pain, but a complete state of physical, emotional, mental and spiritual wellbeing. Living in a world as fast, busy, polluted and stress-filled as ours, it may seem difficult to achieve and maintain health and inner peace. However, it is indeed possible!

Let's start with our thoughts. Everything that humankind has achieved was first a thought in someone's mind. Our thoughts and emotions shape all areas of our lives, mainly our health and wellbeing. We are repeatedly using our thoughts unfavorably, compromising our health as a result of it.

Creation is a process that starts in the mind, and health is definitely something great for us to create. YOU CAN - and YOU SHOULD - use the power of your thoughts to improve your life. In order to do it, you should be aware of the following Universal Laws & Principles:

PRINCIPLE OF SELF-RECOVERY – The body has an innate ability to heal itself at a certain rate. Medicines, doctors, therapists and practitioners of the healing arts just assist in this process by accelerating this innate ability.

PRINCIPLE OF ENERGY FORCE – for life to exist, the body must have energy. Energy can be used in order to accelerate the healing process.
- Everything that exists is an energy
- Energy follows thoughts
- You become what you think of
- You magnify that which you think

PRINCIPLE OF THOUGHT FORMS – Thoughts exist as an energy
- Words are spoken thoughts, thoughts in action

PRINCIPLE OF CAUSE AND EFFECT:
- Everything you do will come back to you magnified many times. You are responsible for what you create and thoughts are creations.
- Like attracts like. Negative thoughts, words and actions will attract negative outcomes and situations. Wholesome thoughts, words and actions will attract positive outcomes.

To take part in the creative process of our lives, we must become aware of our words and thought patterns. Based on the Universal Laws and Principles stated above, we should take responsibility and action in creating our own lives. This does not mean that we dishonor the inner development of events, or that we can get away with our past improper actions that may have produced illness or discomfort; neither does it mean that we dishonor a Divine Higher Power – for those of us who believe. It just means that we can participate in the process of creation, soften the penance and create new, positive karma which will help us in days to come. It means that we choose not to continue creating negativities, and we agree not to be part of that which is not wholesome!

Using constructive affirmations is a very powerful tool that will help us in shaping our health. Continuous positive thoughts become new "programs," which will create positive outcomes, becoming a fountain of well being.

As opposed to thinking "I am sick," it is better to say the same in a more constructive way: "I am in the process of getting better." Not a lie, but a powerful creative, proactive affirmation! Think and affirm "I AM HEALTHY!" Why? Because by doing so you are actually identifying with the real YOU. Since you are not only your body, emotions or thoughts and, since you are a powerful being using these as vehicles, by saying "I AM HEALTHY" you are indeed identifying with that powerful being - with the soul, with the universe. By saying "I AM SICK" you are identifying instead with that which is not true – for the soul is never sick.

By saying "I HAVE A TERRIBLE HEADACHE," you are affirming that you, the one that controls and moves the head, has a headache! In reality, it is not you with a headache, it is indeed the body! Your body! Not YOU. You, the soul, do not have a headache. The soul can't have a headache! By saying "I AM SAD" you are actually declaring that you yourself are sadness, instead of your emotions experiencing sadness. You, the soul, are not sad, or sick, unlucky or terrible! By affirming what is not true your energy will decrease, compromising your body's ability to fight sickness or disease.

Think about how many times in one day you say things like "I can't do it," "I won't get better," "I feel terrible," or "I won't make it." You are giving your power away! You are actually helping the process of getting sicker and feeling worse! If you don't believe it, ponder on this: are you feeling any better? No? Then change the content of the technique you are using! Because as a matter of fact, you are already using a powerful technique: *affirmations!* Same technique, same power, just different content. Give it a try - IT WILL WORK!!!

It doesn't matter whether you believe it or not! JUST REPEAT IT! Even if mechanical, you are creating an energy. The more you say it, the more effective it'll be, and by the law of cause and effect, the more you'll attract it, therefore, the more you'll start believing it! Regardless of our inability to see the air, it is there! Whether you believe it or not, the law of gravity exists...if you throw something, by the law of gravity, it will fall. Period. In the same way, you don't have to believe this: just try it. "You become what you think." It is a law!

Energy is like muscles. It has to be built. You must persevere and persist with your affirmations. Yet don't become fanatical. Keep living a normal life. No need to write down each affirmation 2000 times. No need to surround yourself with so many post-it notes. Just keep a simple yet consistent pace.

The Power of YES

"Yes!" is much more than a powerful affirmation; it is a state of being. It means we are open and receptive to the blessings of life. Say YES to health, Yes to inner peace, Yes to love and Yes to all great things and all great people in life. Most of the time we are not receptive to what we most need or want, and we repeatedly say NO. An example is when someone offers help and the other answers, "No, it's OK, I'll deal with it," instead of saying "Yes, thank you, I appreciate it."

Also, get rid of all the "but's" and "what if's" that often come after a "YES," and just plainly say YES.

Repeatedly use this affirmation:

> "I AM COMPLETELY OPEN AND RECEPTIVE TO HEALTH,
> I WELCOME HEALTH AND INNER PEACE IN MY LIFE."

Imagine yourself healthy and repeatedly say YES to this vision.

Dealing with Negative Thoughts

At the beginning it may be difficult, for you have to fight the tremendous amount of negative thoughts coming from you and others. This is normal. As much as you create positive thoughts, you must also start clearing the way by getting rid of negative thought patterns coming from you or from others. By doing so, your negative thoughts and words will become less frequent and your mental and creative process will become clearer and sharper, which will result in a faster manifestation of your thoughts and words.

Every time you realize that you've said or thought something negative about your health and well being, you should stop and erase this form of energy. I'm sure you've heard people saying "cancel" or "erase" just right after they've said something negative. This is a good step towards dealing with our negative thoughts and words, but it is not enough. Canceling in this way does not deal with the energy created. Use your own energy and creative visualizations to disintegrate the thought-form created and then substitute with a positive thought. This works for all negative patterns of thoughts like fear, jealously, sadness, anger, even stress. For example, to clean fear, substitute with faith and trust.

Creative Visualizations are a very developed way of affirmation that, when properly done, involve energy. The following are a group of powerful visualizations for you to use when negative thoughts come your way. Do them as soon as you have the negative thought. The sooner you do it, the more effective it will be.

1. Be aware of your breathing. This will promote stillness and increase your energy level.

2. Do deep slow abdominal breathing and hold your breath before and after inhalation. Do this for several breathing cycles.

3. Remember you are not your body, emotions or thoughts. You are a being of light, love and power. You are the soul. Mentally affirm this.

4. While continuing to be aware of your breathing, imagine, visualize or have the intention of one of the following:

   a. White Board: Imagine the negative thought, fear or pattern on **a white board.** Then imagine and **have the intention** that you have an eraser made of light in your hands. Erase. Then imagine on the same white board the contrary or positive thought. I.e., if you are stressed, see yourself stressed on the white board, with as much detail as possible. Erase it, then see yourself enjoying life, happy and relaxed.

   b. Ocean of Light: Imagine that you are swimming within an ocean of light, and the waves of light wash the fears, negative thoughts or patterns from you. You can also imagine the negative thoughts in the sand. As the waves come, these thoughts are washed away, leaving behind the positive ones.

   c. Waterfall of Light: Imagine you are under a waterfall of white light. Have the intention that all fear, negative thoughts or patterns are flushed away by it.

   d. Small Fire: Imagine there is a small fire in front of you; use your breathing to exhale the negative thoughts to the flames. While you inhale be aware of the inner stillness and the positive thoughts.

www.mentorsmagazine.com

5. Think of the positive outcome you want to achieve. In this case, think of your health and wellbeing. Think of it as if it was an energy, or a scent. Intentionally inhale this healthy energy into your system while mentally or verbally affirming: "I AM HEALTHY, I AM STRONG, I AM HAPPY. I AM FULL OF LOVE AND LIGHT." You may continue letting go of negative thoughts or patterns by exhaling them after each of these inhalations. Always end the exercise by inhaling the positive energy.

6. Give thanks.

Other Tools to Assist You

Aside from your thoughts, you could also use other tools that are very powerful and of which you can take advantage:

- Practice a form of meditation to achieve inner peace and manage stress.

- Prayer – It has been scientifically proven that those who pray or are prayed for heal faster. Faith plays an important role. It increases the amount of divine energy within and around you, therefore highly accelerating the process of recovering. As you tune in and pray, give thanks for what you want, as if you have it already. Imagine it happening and offer this to The Divine.

- Breathing Exercise. There is a series of breathing exercises that could help you increase your ability to fight sickness. Proper breathing increases your energy level, cleanses and energizes your energy body and boosts your immune system. Start by becoming aware of your breathing. Breathe slowly and deeply. Hold between inhalation and exhalations. For better results, use breathing in combination with creative visualizations.

- Tune in with the pain and ponder the reasons why you could possibly have it and what could you learn from the experience. Once learned, the pain will start dissipating.

- Create positive karma through tithing and service – extreme cases may require extreme measures. When confronted by a major sickness, remember the law: "It is in giving that you receive." Tithe to a good cause and have the intention that it will come back to you in the form of health.

- Create a positive healthy environment, surround yourself with positive, happy and supportive people, and let go of bad habits. Remember, your attitudes shape you.

- Smile...smiling opens up your heart energy center. Your heart energy center controls the thymus gland, which is in charge of the immune system. No wonder happy people tend to be healthy! SMILE!

Finally, Let Me Try to Inspire You...

BELIEVE and GO BACK TO LIVING! There are plenty of people that don't believe, plenty of people that don't have faith and have lost hope. We live in such a fast world that we've almost forgotten the basics, the foundations. Don't be part of it. Don't be just one more. BELIEVE! Develop your inner powers and sense of inner peace. Start living again!

SLOW DOWN: How sad we've become as a race, walking almost as machines, doing without stopping, getting stressed out and always on the run. How did we learn this? When did we forget? Are you enjoying the path? No project is truly important if the price to pay is your inner and outer wellbeing. It's too high of a price. Never compromise your inner peace and inner beauty. Never sacrifice your true being. At the end, it is not going to be about how many miles you ran, how many people you defeated, how much you stressed out, or how much money you accumulated. None of that matters. That last moment, when you are just in front of the soul, what will matter is only whether you learned the lessons and enjoyed the ride.

Start now using your powerful affirmations and welcome to a new healthier YOU!

These principles are not intended to replace orthodox medicine, but to complement it.

Alejandra is a Personal Coach, Mentor, and bi-lingual International Speaker and Writer. She is also a Senior Certified Energy Healer and Senior Instructor of Grand Master Choa Kok Sui's teachings – whose principles she uses and personifies. Alejandra is currently based in Los Angeles, CA. For more information please go to www.manifestingsuccess.com or call 310-995-9039.

The Minerals
of Your Life

By Ann Louise Gittleman, Ph.D., C.N.S.

Here's the best-kept secret in nutrition: minerals are the spark of life and are even more important than vitamins. You see, plants manufacture vitamins but minerals must be obtained from the soil – and minerals are NOT as abundant in the soil anymore. This is why EVERYBODY needs to know about minerals.

The secret – that minerals are more important than vitamins – has been under wraps for nearly 65 years. According to an overlooked document issued by the U.S. Senate in 1936, "Our physical well being is more directly dependent upon minerals we take into our systems than upon calories or vitamins, or upon the precise proportion of starch, protein or carbohydrate we consume." U.S. Senate, Document No. 264, published, 1936.

Many of us are aware we can live for a prolonged period without food – but NOT without water. This is because water provides us with the minerals of life. Let me take you on an abbreviated Magical Mystery Tour of what minerals can do for you.

Besides their role in promoting blood formation, fluid regulation, protein metabolism and energy production, minerals are also co-factors for enzyme catalysts for every biochemical response in the body. Can you guess which mineral is involved in over 350 biochemical processes like muscle contraction, nerve conduction, and the prevention of anxiety, irritability, asthma and panic attacks? It's widely considered the most important mineral in the body. All of the other major minerals (like calcium, potassium and sodium) are dependent upon its presence in order to function.

It's Magnesium.

Even sleep can be affected by the lack of magnesium. People who are magnesium deficient tend to fall asleep readily but wake up periodically. They toss and turn and wake up exhausted. I recommend keeping a bottle of magnesium right on your bed stand. Magnesium is designed to support nighttime rest or occasional sleeplessness.

Now try this one: which mineral is involved in over 100 biochemical processes like the stimulation of taste, smell, wound healing, immunity and the maintenance of thick hair (without split ends) and enhancement of healthy blood sugar levels? If you guessed zinc, you're right on.

Minerals also maintain strong bones and teeth. But not just with calcium, also with magnesium. In fact, the research of Dr. Mildred Seelig – widely recognized as the most distinguished magnesium expert in the U.S. – suggests that a 1:1 ratio of both calcium and magnesium is essential for bones, teeth and the prevention of hypertension and hardening of the arteries.

Excess calcium – without equal amounts of magnesium – can result in calcified arteries and heart valves, migraines, cataracts, gallstones, kidney stones and irritability. Some researchers even suggest that a 2:1 ratio in favor of magnesium to calcium is even better for overall health, including bone density.

Magnesium gives your bones the flexibility and strength of ivory. Ivory is a combination of 50 percent magnesium and about 50 percent calcium. Chalk, on the other hand, is 100 percent calcium and looks dense on the outside but is very porous and weak and easily breakable.

The moral of the story is calcium should not be taken on its own. If it is, it will pull magnesium out of body parts in order to assimilate it, creating a further magnesium deficiency.

Minerals maintain organ and glandular strength. The liver's key minerals – the body's head honchos for detoxification of all wastes – are potassium and sulfur. The liver contains twice as much potassium as sodium. Sulfur is an important nutrient because it's needed to make glutathione, the liver's most important antioxidant for neutralizing those nasty free radicals associated with every degenerative disease from cancer to heart disease.

The thyroid gland needs both iodine and selenium to make thyroid hormones while the adrenals need zinc for the production of adrenal cortical hormones.

Think Zinc!

Minerals can support mood and relieve stress and frustration. The copper-zinc ratio is *the* most important ratio when it comes to behavior. Elevated copper and deficient zinc have been associated with hyperactivity, Attention Deficit Disorder, violence and depression. The Pfeiffer Treatment Center in Naperville, Illinois has found that 80 percent of hyperactive patients and 68 percent of behavior disordered patients have elevated blood copper levels.

Many high copper depressives experience severe post-menopausal syndrome, are intolerant to estrogen and have a family history of post partum depression. This group also has a high incidence of acne, eczema, sensitive skin, sunburn, headaches and white spots on their fingernails. The ideal ratio of zinc to copper in the blood stream is 8:1.

Minerals are your body's batteries and spark plugs. There are over 70 trillion cells in the body and each is like a biological battery – a mini dynamo that generates life. Minerals are the catalysts to keep the battery going and to hold a charge. Without minerals in the proper ratio, your cellular membranes can't maintain the proper liquid pressure between the inside and outside cell walls. Without this balance, the cells become weak and eventually die. Your immune system depends upon this mineral balancing act right down to the cellular level.

Remember that without the battery and spark plugs, even the most expensive automobile won't run. The minerals of life recharge us on a minute by minute, daily basis empowering every cell, organ and tissue of the body.

So, Where Did All the Minerals Go?

We need to get our minerals from the water we drink and the food we eat. The problem is as a result of past and present farming methods, there are virtually NO nutritional minerals in our farm and range soils today. As a result, the crops that are grown are mineral deficient and the animals and people who eat these mineral deficient crops get sick. Many of today's long term degenerative diseases like arthritis, heart disease, hypertension and arteriosclerosis are caused by nutritional deficiencies. Now you can add asthma, irritability and anxiety to the mix.

A fascinating study at the Earth Summit in Rio De Janeiro in June 1992 compared the mineral content of soils today with soils 100 years ago. Researchers found that in African soils there were 74 percent less minerals present in the soil today then there were 100 years ago. Asian soils had 76 percent less, European soils 72 percent less, and South American soils 76 percent less. Soils in the U.S. and Canada contained 85 percent less minerals than they did 100 years ago.

Additional data compiled by Paul Bergner of Boulder, Colorado shows the disappearance of minerals from our soil graphically. Bergner compared data from 1914, 1948 and 1992. Besides soil depletion, minerals get axed due to other factors like stress, drug interactions, coffee, alcohol, sugar, excessive grains and heavy metals. Let's take a look at these:

- Stress – Hans Selye, M.D., a pioneer in stress research found that stress – whether from lack of sleep, injury, pollution, or from stimulants like coffee, sugar and drugs – will cause the body to lose minerals even more than vitamins. The key minerals most affected by stress are magnesium, calcium, zinc, potassium, sodium and copper.

- Drug Interactions – Many drugs can severely restrict the percentage of minerals we get from the foods we eat. In fact, some drugs reduce mineral absorption as much as tenfold. The birth control pill interferes with both zinc and selenium absorption, which can lead to memory loss, muscle weakness and weakened immunity. Hormone replacement therapy, like Premarin, can leave you short of magnesium. No wonder women report side effects like depression and muscle cramps. Antacids that contain aluminum disturb both calcium and magnesium metabolism. Diuretics, as well as antibiotics, are notorious for flushing potassium out of the body, leaving your muscles tight and tense. Cortisone, Tagamet and Zantac impair zinc absorption, making you susceptible to viruses and anxiety. In fact, in many holistic circles, zinc is known as the "good-mood" mineral.

- Coffee, Alcohol, Sugar, Excess Grains – These popular food and beverage robbers are major mineral thieves. Calcium, as well as other important minerals like magnesium, are lost in the urine when you drink coffee and/ or alcohol. Caffeine is so diuretic it alone doubles the rate of calcium excretion. A mere three cups of black coffee can result in a 45 mg loss of calcium – and women between the ages of 35 and 50 drink more coffee than any other age group. Sugar robs us more because in the process of being metabolized, refined sugar uses our magnesium, manganese, chromium, zinc and vanadium. Grains contain phytic acid – a phosphorus-like compound that combines with calcium in the intestine and blocks its absorption. Grains can also provide too much insoluble fiber, which binds with and sweeps out minerals like manganese and zinc from the body.

- Heavy Metals – When it comes to heavy metals, minerals can really save the day. Toxic metals – those unbound, electro-magnetically active ions – are everywhere. Space does not permit to discuss all the heavy metals, but here are two of the most insidious and ubiquitous – mercury and aluminum – which researchers have suggested are at the root of a myriad of disorders.

  - Mercury – Found in large fish like tuna and swordfish, silver amalgam fillings, water supplies, seeds treated with mercurial fungicides, vaccines including both infant and adult vaccines, eyedrops and contact lense solutions (thimerosal), nasal sprays, eardrops and hemorrhoid creams. Classified as a poison because it is a neurotoxin and irreversibly blocks protein synthesis. The main target organs and glands for mercury are the kidneys, thyroid and pituitary. The most threatening mercury compound is organic methylmercury. The minerals selenium and zinc are both antagonists to mercury toxicity. Metabolic dysfunctions associated with mercury toxicity include:

    1. Alopecia (hair loss) – causes impairment of copper Metabolism
    2. Excessive salivation
    3. Vision loss
    4. Ataxia – failure of muscular coordination, muscle weakness, numbness and tingling, tremors
    5. Birth defects – higher incidence of cerebral palsy, mental retardation and neurological deficits
    6. Infertility
    7. Hearing Loss – mercury has an affinity for the acoustic nerve
    8. Depression – accumulation in the thyroid and pituitary glands causing a slowing of the metabolic rate
    9. Memory loss – migraine headaches, mood swings, nervousness
    10. Dermatitis – caused by a mercury-induced zinc depletion
    11. Blushing – rashes
    12. Hyperactivity

www.mentorsmagazine.com

13. Immune system dysfunction resulting in multiple sclerosis

- Aluminum – Found in antacids like Maalox, Mylanta and Gelusil, buffered aspirins, aluminum cookware, cans, antiperspirants and deodorants, cosmetics, water supplies, baking powders, salt and various brands of colloidal minerals. Penetrates the blood-brain barrier accumulating in brain cells, impedes the body's utilization of calcium, phosphorus and magnesium, and neutralizes the protein-digesting enzyme pepsin in the stomach. Magnesium and selenium are aluminum's mineral antagonists. Calcium is another healing mineral that counteracts metal toxicity – the mineral antagonist to lead and excess iron. Metabolic dysfunctions potentially associated with aluminum toxicity include:

1. Alzheimer's disease – dementia
2. Kidney and liver dysfunction
3. Neuromuscular disorders – possible link with Parkinson's disease
4. Amyotrophic lateral sclerosis
5. Anemia – due to the interference of aluminum with iron metabolism
6. Colic – affects bowel activity and can cause digestive disturbances
7. Dental carries – impairs bone calcification and competes with
   natural fluoride
8. Fibromyalgia

New Horizons in Mineral Research – The Mind, Body, Spirit Connection

By far, the most exciting research today is being conducted at the Pfeiffer Institute where they are exploring the origins of behavior. Pfeiffer researchers feel that violent behavior may not be just a matter of genes or upbringing, but may be more related to nutritional imbalances.

In a study published in the journal *Physiology and Behavior*, Dr. William Walsh of the Pfeiffer Institute compared results of blood tests given to 135 assaultive men to those of 18 controls with no history of violence. It turned out the violent young men had lower zinc and higher copper levels than the control group.

The more imbalanced the ratio, the more severe the frequency of aggression. When the young men were given extra zinc in the form of supplementation, their violent episodes substantially declined.

I guess you could say, "A Deficiency Made Me Do It" – and zinc is probably one of the three most deficient minerals in our diet today, a shame because zinc plays a significant role in brain function and well being. It is a mood-supporting nutrient.

The Pfeiffer Institute also made headlines when Dr. Walsh released the results of his heavy metal evaluation of Beethoven's hair. Walsh discovered more than 100 times the amount of lead in the famed composer's locks. The lead toxicity is now believed to be the underlying cause of Beethoven's deafness and irrational behavior. Today we know lead binds to phospholipids of the nervous membrane. Toxic amounts of lead in children have been associated with a reduced IQ, hyperactivity, inability to concentrate and learning difficulties. Other minerals you will be hearing about in the years ahead include:

- Sulfur for pain management, and as an anti-arthritic agent

- Vanadium, chromium and zinc as insulin – co-factors and potent nutritional therapy for diabetes, low blood sugar and Syndrome X. The mysterious sounding Syndrome X, a term coined by Stanford University's Dr. Gerald Reaven, refers to a group of health problems including insulin resistance (the inability to properly metabolize sugars), elevated cholesterol and triglycerides, weight problems and high blood pressure.

Tomorrow's Health Today

The right mineral balance will provide you with tomorrow's health remedies today! One of the very best, non-invasive ways to assess your personal mineral needs is through mineral tissue analysis via a tablespoon or two of your hair. Uni Key, the official distributor of all of my products, books and services, offers hair analysis through an FDA approved and regulated laboratory (800-888-4353 OR www.unikeyhealth.com). In closing, I believe that health is God's greatest gift to us. Health is that which we use up for the first 60 years of life in order to obtain wealth, after which we use up our wealth to try and recapture our lost health! Minerals can lead the way.

Ann Louise Gittleman, Ph.D., C.N.S., is continually breaking new ground in health and healing – from natural hormone replacement to effective, safe and cleansing weight loss. An award-winning author of 20 books with over 3.5 million copies in print, her latest New York Times bestsellers are *Before the Change* and *The Fat Flush Plan*. For more, visit www.fatflush.com.

Photo by Jonathan Exley, © 2003 EXLEY-FOTO, inc.

Being Your Best
at Any Age

By Dr. Marcus Laux

Having the best of health can be achieved, but it is not a given. I believe that for most of us, good health before the age of 35 is what we inherited through our genes while our health thereafter comes more from how we choose to live. Yet, with all of today's complexities, demanding schedules, fake fast foods and technological trappings, it is challenging to make the time for our first priority, our greatest of wealths – our health.

All aspects considered, your strongest health insurance comes from pulling the plug on stress, eating less and moving more. The healthiest people in the world all have this in common: they lead more simple lives. Regardless of personal income and social status, they've made a choice to live a life that is arguably more deeply rewarding and personally satisfying. A life filled with realizing hopes and dreams, as opposed to a life chasing questionable ones. A quality of life and health earned each day, not borrowed heavily against for a promised payoff some day to come.

Strong Genes Help Less Than We Thought

Genes factor into our health equation far less than was previously thought. While great genes are a plus, it is our internal environment that dictates how and what gets produced from our genes. They can be turned on and off by our diet and lifestyle. Genes have the ability – in fact, a DNA mandate – to make a variety of proteins, depending on the signals and environment they are immersed in. It is our day-to-day living that mostly determines this, and it's our habits and practices, far more than any other factors, that create our health, our predisposition to disease or ageless longevity. There is no magic potion or new product that will ever replace the power of your daily decisions, actions and habits to engender health. You alone have the awesome power to change your health experience in the world.

Mind and Body Are Equally Important

The mind and body are inextricably linked – it is impossible and indeed futile to determine where the one ends and the other begins. They are both irreplaceable parts of a larger whole. We are simultaneously both a body of energy, with thousands of electrical firings per second in the neurons of our brains and spinal cord, and a sophisticated, adaptive, biological organism pre-programmed to survive. We are a spectacular blend of electrical, magnetic and biochemical biology that interplays, interacts and self-adjusts, if given the opportunity. All healing modalities, from meditation to surgery, strive to create the right environment, the right opportunity, for us to self-adjust to a higher vibration of health.

Just as our external environment affects our health, our thoughts and feelings – conscious and unconscious – play significant roles in our unfolding health every moment. They impact us as powerfully as our physical and environmental encounters do.

You Can Change Your Mind Anytime

Our needs and desires, our emotions and thoughts, equally influence our health. Our relationship with ourselves is delicate and needs nourishing and balance, so critical in a speeding world much out of balance. Slow down, unplug the noise and get in touch with what you know you want and need to do for you. We all know what we need to do, but we have excuses, reasons, expectations or blind spots.

So, when is it time for you to declare your needs? I say now. You decide, but don't wait too long. Being selfish can be a very good thing. Saying 'no' can be the best response given when it respects you. Taking a second, a day, a week off, to get back on track can rekindle your spirit.

It's Never Too Late to Change

Good intentions followed by changes are paramount to ensuring health. It is the commitment to your plans, your beliefs and consistent action to that end that delivers your desires, and promotes and protects your health at every age. It is never too late to start right now, right where you are, to create the health you want. We are all programmed to respond and adapt. The notion of old age meaning advanced decrepitude is outdated, based on lack of knowledge. Aches and pains and loss of function are not inevitable – in fact, they are flat-out avoidable. I've worked with a man who at 55 years old had diabetes, heart disease, hypertension, arthritis and obesity. He drank, smoked, worked a high stress job and ate poorly. He needed to take charge of his health, or he was going to die sooner rather than later. He did take charge, and last I knew, at 68 years of age he was cycling across America, and was off all medication. He created a new vision, set new goals and, with God's grace, made himself into a completely renewed person. What's your vision?

Eat Real Food

What you eat, and how much, is the foundation to bulletproof health. From studying healthy long-lived peoples around the globe, as well as from animal studies on longevity, it is clear that eating high quality foods, rich in nutrients, yet lower in calories, creates the optimal setting for achieving lasting health, greater life spans and less disease. And it is possible to be fully functional, intact and sharp-witted with keen eyesight for your entire life-trip. Recent evidence now puts our potential life-span at around 150 years old. Some animals may live to be 1,000 years old. Better genes, maybe, but superb food, no junk, regular movement and lower stress – you bet.

Yes, You Are What You Eat

You are what you are from the food that is consumed. Life feeds life. There is no way around this simple, yet profound, fact. Eat bad fats, and every cell is set up to falter. Eat sugar, and you imbalance your hormones and dull your immunity. Eat junk, and you create a paler, weaker version of what you are meant to be.

Eat organic fresh foods, some cooked, some raw, seasonally and locally when possible, and watch yourself rejuvenate, replenish and renew. The killer diseases of today are chronic and degenerative. 'Chronic' simply means that it is ongoing, in large part due to our everyday diets and environmental exposure. 'Degenerative' means we are slowly falling apart because we are not maintaining, replenishing and renewing by providing what our bodies need to thrive. The missing ingredients are from the farm, not the pharmacy.

Take Time to Smell the Roses

Stress is a fact of life. Let it be a friend in your health, and not a factor in your disease. Stress can motivate your behavior, and even improve your performance. Choose your stresses, and deal with them as tasks to be handled and accounts to be settled. You control stress by using it as an opportunity, a challenge and a priority. We all must learn what we have control over and what we don't. Stress has no control over us, unless we so empower it. This also means you can neuter it. Stress is not your boss, but a masquerading wannabe. Choose instead to make it an ally.

Accept Limitations

You can only do so much in a day. Let the rest go. Work smarter, work better and then stop. Make technology work for you. Use your phones, pagers and computers to free your time for living. They can be a leash of limitations or a new lease on freedom.

Go spend time with your friends, family and yourself. Play fun and fully. Rest well and deeply. Leave the stress behind – don't carry it from one to the other. Just put it on your list at work, and when ready, take it up and make your best efforts. At the end of your day, leave it on your desk. Do what you can, and leave the rest. Really – release it for now. It will improve your mind, metabolism and your fun factor. When you are living in the moment now, worry has no home.

Check in on Yourself

It is not only what you eat that counts, but *what is eating you* that takes a bite out of your health, mood and energy. How do you know what's in the back of your mind? Here are a few clues. What do you think about when driving? What pops into your head as you are falling asleep, or as you wake? What's on your mind when you are taking a shower? Or looking in the mirror? Anything less than love, respect and acceptance of yourself is a red flag. It is so interesting that we can see every part of our body, except our face, the part to which we all attach our identity, and often so much more. We need something that is not us, to tell us about the 'face' we put out to the world – a mirror, a friend, a parent, a teacher, coach, a passer-by. Examining yourself *by yourself* can reveal many places to start to grow healthier than ever before. Get to know yourself.

Find What Moves You and Do It

Just look at your body. A most obvious fact is, pound for pound, we are mostly muscle and bone. We were given amazing joints, ligaments, tendons and a spine for one thing – to move. We are designed to move, walk, run, jump, dance, swim and stretch. This action is mandatory for our best of health. Moving our bodies does everything good for recovering balance and mood, building all levels of mental and physical health and helping remove the wastes while managing our metabolism. Everything good, nothing bad.

Exercise should not be torture, but movement enjoyed, at your pace and pleasure. It is not about no pain, no gain. Our bodies really appreciate regularity of all kinds, exercise included. Exercise is the celebration of life itself. 'Use it' or 'lose it' should ring a bell here for you. The journey of good health starts with the first step. Exercise can be anything. Discover, uncover or recover exercise that you enjoy, and do it! Stay with it and health will follow as day follows night. Results are measured by the month, not by the numbers on your scale.

Everyday Things Matter

Change your mind about your mind. All lasting improvement and health starts here. Change your mind about disease, as it is really *dis-ease*. Put your body at ease, on the regenerative road to health, and naturally experience one of life's greatest gifts and miracles – healing. In the end, all healing is self-healing. The doctor stitches, the physician prescribes, the bandages protect, but you, the person, heal. The power of your life force, the energy that flows through you like breath through a flute, is strengthened, purified and powered by the vital messages from nature (the nutrients from our diet and clean air) and by your actions (the result of fully vested thoughts and beliefs).

The combination of eating real foods, regular physical exercise performed as part of your daily activities, social involvement and cooperation within a network of friends and associates, with a good share of humor, appears to be the tried and true recipe for healthy living. Being truly connected to yourself, family and friends helps insure good health. Life begets life. Life is given through intimate expression, and thrives a lifetime from drinking deeply from the well of personal bonds. Communication expands our heart and soothes our soul. Let it save your life and others as you flower as a friend. Build bridges, not barriers.

Life is not about being perfect, but it is about being purposeful. Do you have a philosophy, a belief system, a game plan for your daily life? Do your actions reflect your beliefs and help you get what you want? This is your litmus test. Physician, heal thyself.

Know yourself. Know where you want to go. Love yourself. Live by your principles. Act your truth. Realize your dreams. Walk with the wise.

Dr. Marcus Laux is a licensed naturopathic physician with a Doctorate from the National College of Naturopathic Medicine in Portland, Oregon. He is an Affiliate Faculty Member of Bastyr University in Kenmore, Washington and editor of *Naturally Well Today*, a monthly newsletter. Learn more about Dr. Laux at www.drmarcuslaux.com.

Swan Lake,
A Chiropractor's Memory
By Dr. Alan Rousso

I remember it like it was yesterday. It was a beautiful spring day and the air was cool and crisp. The sun was shining brightly and families were gathering at Swan Lake for the beginning of the Memorial Day weekend and the start of summer vacation at the bungalow colony.

Grandpa particularly loved this time of year. The water at the pool was still ice cold and no one dared to go into the water yet... except Grandpa. You see, Grandpa loved to swim in ice cold water and the opportunity to be the first one into the pool invigorated him.

As Grandpa jumped into the pool, the icy water embraced his strong, muscular body and made him feel young and vibrant. Other family members would gather with delight as they watched Grandpa swim with such effortless power and grace.

I was Grandpa's first grandchild. At the time, I was only two years old and this was the first time in my young life that I would be able to walk over to the pool to watch Grandpa swim. Nothing could have excited Grandpa more than to see his first and only grandson smile and giggle, as he would swim laps around the pool.

When Grandpa stopped swimming, I wanted to be with him. The sound of the family's laughter, the splashing of the clear blue water and this unusually beautiful sunny day were just too much excitement for me to take. I jumped into the water to be with Grandpa and there was an immediate *shock* to my nervous system.

The icy water was much too cold for my fragile body. Between the effect of the frigid temperature and the swallowing of the pool water, I gasped for air as the family stared and screamed in horror.

Grandpa immediately rushed to my sickening cry, grabbed me and jumped out of the pool with me in his arms. All seemed well as I choked and coughed and then started to smile with Grandpa by my side.

But a week later, I developed a severe cough. The shock on my nervous system from jumping into the frigid water had taken its toll. A local pediatrician

33

examined me and diagnosed pneumonia. The family had to drive all the way back to New York to see our esteemed pediatrician, Dr. Shein, upon the local doctor's recommendation.

After examining me, Dr. Shein confirmed it was indeed a case of severe pneumonia. He prescribed antibiotics, assured the family all would be well, and instructed us to return to Swan Lake for the rest of the summer vacation.

After 10 days of taking the antibiotics, my pneumonia was a thing of the past. The memory of that horrible incident all but passed and life resumed back to normal.

Had the antibiotics taken care of the cause of my pneumonia, or was there something more insidious that had affected my health? That question could only be answered years later, because I developed asthma just a few short weeks after summer vacation was over.

Two years passed and now I was four years old. The asthmatic attacks that I was suffering from just seemed to be getting worse, coming on more frequently and lasting longer. The inhalant, intended to control the wheezing (Isuprel Mistometer), was also being used more often. Although the attacks would subside with the medication, the physical condition of my health was clearly deteriorating.

Some three more years passed and at the impressionable age of seven, I knew I was not like other boys. They would play baseball and dodge ball during recreation at school, while I would sit by myself...not allowed to play because this would aggravate my condition and cause me to wheeze. Classmates would tease and shout names while I would cry or distract myself from their taunts and laughter.

Periodic trips to the hospital for Adrenalin shots were now also part of the needed treatment to quell my attacks. Exhaustive evenings were spent on midnight car rides with air conditioning to avoid the effects of the hot and damp night air since my home had no air-conditioning. It was now apparent this condition was getting worse and nothing seemed to be able help.

Another check-up at the pediatrician's office revealed that I was developing a barrel chest and enlarged heart. Blood tests revealed the years of antibiotics were beginning to take a toll on my kidneys. The only solution was to now give me cortisone.

This new drug cortisone was supposed to work wonders on asthmatic conditions and it sounded like a perfect solution. My father thought this was a better answer than to move the entire family to Colorado or Arizona for a new environment so I could breathe.

My mother, Phyllis, was not so sure. There were serious side effects to this new drug cortisone and the cure could be worse than the disease! After all, I had been taking medication for five years now, and nothing was better, in fact, it was worse. There had to be a better way.

––––––––––––

Aunt Thelma stepped into the chiropractor's office for the first time. She was nervous about this "doctor" because she had never heard of a chiropractor before. She had heard chiropractors weren't even licensed in New York in 1961, but offered help and relief for her painful slipped disc that regular medical doctors could not.

After only a few office visits, her pain and stiffness disappeared. Aunt Thelma was very impressed by this outgoing, young and flamboyant Dr. Klein, as he proceeded to tell her how and why she felt so much better from what was known as an *adjustment*.

"You see," Dr. Klein explained, "many problems begin because of trauma or stress on the nervous system causing nerve interference, also known as a subluxation. By eliminating nerve interference with a light thrust to the spine known as an adjustment, the normal nerve impulses are restored and the body is able to heal itself." This made sense to Aunt Thelma and she thought of her nephew who was suffering with asthma. Could chiropractic care help him?

Later that day, Aunt Thelma explained chiropractic care to my mother. It seemed like the answer to her prayers. She immediately called the chiropractor's office and made an appointment, but there was one problem – my father, Bob.

My father was not about to allow his oldest son to visit some quack. He had heard that chiropractors hurt people and that they weren't even licensed. This was enough reason to stand at the doorway to prevent my mom and I from leaving the house for the chiropractor's office.

My mom, however, would not be deterred. She immediately went to the kitchen, drew a kitchen knife from the drawer and said, "Bob, get out of my way or I'll stab you through the heart." My dad could tell my mom was more than serious and stepped aside as we headed toward the chiropractor's office.

––––––––––––

The chiropractor, Dr. Klein, examined me and found that I had a subluxation at the T3, T4 level of the spine. This was the area of the spine that was

responsible for heart and lung function and that function was being compromised from this nerve interference. My mother was shocked and dismayed that no one had told her this before. Why did her son have to suffer for so many years, when the answer seemed so apparent? She immediately started me on a course of chiropractic care after Dr. Klein confirmed that I was a chiropractic case.

The results were dramatic! My nails that were perpetually blue turned pink after my first adjustment. My lips that were always a tinge of blue also turned to a vibrant shade of pink – all this just after the first adjustment.

I slept peacefully that evening for the first time in years and continued to sleep for the next 24 hours – a welcome relief from the endless sleepless nights and frequent trips to the hospital and midnight car rides.

After a few months of chiropractic care, my physical condition began to improve! The attacks were far less frequent and much shorter in duration. Even when I needed the inhalant, it now seemed to be able to control the wheezing while the chiropractic care was helping me and my asthmatic condition heal.

The chiropractor then informed my mother that it was time to change my *lifestyle*. His first recommendation was to encourage me to play with the other children in my grade and to start exercising again. Exercise would be necessary to strengthen my weakened frame. I was ecstatic to learn that I could play again. I had also gained a tremendous amount of weight during those long years of suffering and struggling to breathe and was very out of shape.

My mom became uneasy about my exercising because it might aggravate my condition that would cause me to wheeze. The chiropractor understood her concern and assured her this was a necessary step to begin to strengthen my fragile body and to start losing the weight that I had gained from both inactivity and all the medications I had been taking.

I also had a horrible diet and the chiropractor was very clear that my diet had to change immediately. Fresh fruits, lean meats and vegetables were to replace sugared cereals and canned goods, along with supplements, and the elimination of dairy products.

Two years passed and slowly but surely, my physical condition was changing – for the better. Even the pediatrician was amazed at how the lungs were sounding clearer and my body was looking closer to the way a normal nine-year-old's should. I was lean, muscular and even my attitude improved. No longer was I worried about being a respiratory cripple or dying at an early age as I was once informed I would by the pediatrician.

Entering into adolescence, I continued to go to the chiropractor, not only for asthma, but because my overall health just kept improving. My chiropractor served as a role model, too and encouraged me to join his track team when I entered junior high school. I followed my chiropractor's advice and went on to join the gymnastics team, too.

When it was time to enter college, I decided to major in biology – a pre-requisite necessary to enter Chiropractic College. I started New York Chiropractic College in 1976 and didn't suffer from another asthmatic attack ever again. I graduated in 1979 and went on to private practice in Brooklyn, New York for almost 10 years and helped many people with a variety of conditions.

Among my favorite patients were young boys and girls who suffered from allergies and asthma. They too would see the amazing results that a course of chiropractic care could offer. Many of these patients were referred from a nurse working at Coney Island Hospital who was a patient of mine who also suffered from asthma – but this is just the beginning of the story.

You see, I sold my practice in 1990 after 10 years and joined a consulting group known as Markson Management Services, to consult with other chiropractors. Over the years, I have been able to influence hundreds and hundreds of other chiropractors to help them and their patients attain better lives through chiropractic care.

The group grew and evolved to now be known as "The Masters Circle." In addition to coaching and consulting, I am a renowned public speaker who continues to help transform lives, just as mine was transformed so many years ago.

This story clearly represents not only how a lifestyle of exercise, proper nutrition and chiropractic care can change the lives of people in our society, but more importantly, how one idea, one referral, can change the course of hundreds and hundreds of lives for years to come.

"You never know how far reaching something you say or do can affect the lives of others."

– B.J. Palmer, DC, PHC

Dr. Alan Rousso is a Senior Consultant and featured speaker for
The Masters Circle, one of the world's largest Personal
Development and Practice Building companies for
Chiropractors. For the past 13 years, he has managed
and coached over 2,000 Chiropractic offices.
He can be reached at 800-451-4514.

www.mentorsmagazine.com

Feed the Body,
Nourish the Soul

By Judy Kay Gray, M.S.

Life is a great gift, a gift with a purpose. That purpose is growing in a good and powerful way. God created all life. Thus, our souls are a bit of God. Some are most grateful for the gift of life and use it well. Others choose to follow a lower path and refuse to see that there are always options.

The spirit has substance. Its energy can be high or low, according to choices made. Researchers found that every person in their study at the time of death lost approximately seven ounces. This seven ounces is energy, and the higher the vibration of that energy, the closer one is to God.

We are born to learn, to make the best choices, and to learn from good and bad choices. Most of all we are born to love. Through love and truly caring, we can change the world.

Today, life energy is out of balance. The proof is the increasing number of people suffering from ailments and diseases, many of them psychological. For example, obesity is pandemic in the United States. One of fifty people is over 100 pounds overweight; two of three are over 10 pounds overweight. Maria eats cake, Laura eats chocolate, Bernie drinks beer, and Paul likes cookies. Treats to be enjoyed occasionally, if at all, are consumed daily. Most people do no hard physical labor to burn calories. Yet, food intake is higher than ever, with disastrous results.

We are a depressed, undernourished, and lovelorn society. This can be proven by television commercials. Commercials give an impression that consuming certain foods will make you attractive and happy. Instead, they make you sick – and fat. Then drugs are advertised for the symptoms. Soon, the body, heart, and soul suffer the consequences.

Eating only for pleasure is disastrous. We eat to still hunger pangs and for fun. Now it's socially acceptable to make fun of wholesome food. One woman stated, "this is just entirely too healthy for me." Teenagers and young adults are setting the stage for the rest of their lives. Bad eating habits become firmly established, and physiology is damaged.

Many have never tasted real food. Modern food is a mixture of refined chemicals with long names, plus, it is usually loaded with sugar and hydrogenated oils. Nutritionally corrupted foods cause our bodies to become malnourished. The result of bad food choices is disease: mainly diabetes, heart disease, or cancer. The health and welfare of the human race is at risk as evidenced by the rising rate of infertility, sudden death, and obesity. Yet, the solution is simple: pure, fresh, unadulterated food and water. This improves life immediately.

The Real Solution? It's Real Food!

What is food? Real food is from plants nourished by the sun and soil. Wild plants must fight for their lives. Compared to commercial foods they are stronger and more nourishing. There are not enough wild plants to feed everyone, but organic, non-genetically engineered food can. Real food picked at its peak and immediately eaten is invigorating. This is how God intended us to be nourished. Our bodies respond rapidly to such a wholesome approach, even those sickened and overweight from chemical overload. Books which give further guidance include Dr. Cass Ingram's *How to Eat Right and Live Longer*, *Supermarket Remedies*, and *Lifesaving Cures*.

Since wild plants have the greatest healing potential, it is ideal to use some every day. I explored over 50 countries, many quite remote. The magnificent plant life there is glowing with color and shimmering with energy. One of the wild plant combinations villagers used for hundreds of years provides tannic, malic, and gallic acids, which vastly improve digestion. In this natural source of calcium, silica, magnesium, and zinc the minerals are easily absorbed. It improves bone density, hair texture, nail strength, and skin. It has natural pain-relieving properties.

When a severe fall caused an excruciatingly painful hip fracture, I took the usual mega-mineral tablets. After choking on those rock-hard monsters, which weren't helping the healing process, I decided to stop forcing them down and try the village miracle food grown out of the calcium-rich rocks. Within four days the pain was gone. Skeptical, I stopped taking it and the pain returned. No further convincing was necessary, and I enjoyed a rapid recovery. Bone density testing proved that my bone mass increased dramatically. Unexpected side effects were the disappearance of colitis and Candida symptoms.

Wild or organic foods are filled with nutrients that speak to the body and then answer its needs. They nourish the nerves and glands by providing high amounts of B vitamins and naturally occurring steroids, minerals, other vitamins and co-factors. Rice polish, brans, sunflower seeds, and nutritional yeast are excellent sources. Other nutrient dense foods come from bees. The bees take nutrients from flower pollen and make a powerful substance called royal jelly. Royal jelly may be processed in ways that affect the quality and purity, so use the highest grade available. Animals, fish, and poultry supply high levels of nutrients, especially from the liver and eggs.

I finally realized how important nutrients in food are during a rigid weight loss diet. The food during my childhood seemed delicious, but it had little nutritional value. As a teenager I gained weight and was always hungry. A rigid high protein, low carbohydrate diet resulted in weight loss. I realized that hunger comes from the body's demand for nutrients. I dropped from a size 16 to a size 2.

So-called food is plentiful in the United States and so are drugs. It's as if people are drug deficient, since they take so many of them. Seventy-five per cent of children are consuming some form of mind-altering chemicals or drugs, when food additives and caffeine are included. Drugs and chemicals deplete critical nutrients. Chemicals also disturb appetite, often accelerating it. Certain chemicals are added to food strictly as appetite stimulants. Such substances disturb the function of all organs, particularly the liver, brain, and kidneys.

Synthetic chemicals and drugs destroy nutrients resulting in severe nutritional deficiency and a wide range of maladies. Lack of B vitamins is the main cause of depression, mental derangement, and nervous disorders. B vitamins control mood. Thus, deficiency can lead to severe agitation, even violence. Children are weakened by poor diets and drug consumption of their parents. An acquaintance gloated that her baby should look like a pizza, because that's what she mostly ate during her pregnancy. Already undernourished children are fed so called kid's food, which is little more than food coloring and polished starches, plus lots of sugar. I witnessed a mother feeding a handful of colorful rubbery candy to a tiny beautiful smiling girl in a stroller. Predictably, within a few minutes she turned into a screaming, stiffened, red-faced monster. Why do this to children? Feed them what their bodies need.

When life isn't sweet enough, people seek temporary pleasures. We pamper ourselves with our addictions. People overwhelm their bodies with chocolate, alcohol, sugar, cigarettes, and every other kind of addiction that can be conceived. Maybe you are an addict. It only takes 21 days for a person to establish an addiction and another 21 days to abolish it. Cold turkey is the best way to cure an addiction. You must be adamant to be cured.

Addiction to cocaine is extremely difficult to cure, but SUGAR abuse is worse. The three top killers, heart disease, cancer, and diabetes, are sugar-induced. Some form of this substance is found in most manufactured foods and many so-called health foods. When you know you have a purpose and an important role – to nourish your vital soul – then it is easy to break the addiction. You will honor your body.

Healthy food feeds both the body and the soul. There is no greater feeling than the warmth of love as it fills the heart and soul. It's difficult to achieve if the body is polluted by noxious foods. Yet, that feeling of warmth in the heart is what every soul craves more than anything. True pure love is worth every effort.

Aberrant and violent actions arise from a lack of the precious commodity: LOVE. Being spiritually fulfilled, nourished by the glow of love and spiritual advancement, our aberrant appetites lessen. When love fills the heart and soul, evil actions are impossible to commit. Thoughts have substance and power and can improve personal growth and the surrounding environment. When a soul, choked with hate, anger, and spite, commits an act against you, only love can block the internal pain that results. If your heart and soul remain filled with love, such negativity is unable to hurt you. Love is the answer.

The Spiritual Diet

Of all energy, love is the highest form with the highest vibration. It can be claimed that truly natural and/or wild food has its own love energy. When corrupted and processed, this energy is lost. This leads us to the spiritual diet. Choosing, preparing, and eating food with joy, passion, and honesty lifts the soul to a higher level. Self-pity and selfishness are the two greatest stumbling blocks, which thoroughly block love energy. Even selfishness regarding food, refusing to share or thinking only about your personal needs, has a negative effect.

A person who is angry or depressed when eating will fail to gain the ideal benefits. Before eating think about what makes you happy and fills your heart with the warmth of love. Make notes, so you can develop it into a pattern. When you think of that which activates the love response, add it to your list. As your love list grows, so will your spirit, and your physical body will become more balanced. Old destructive habits will fade away. YOU will change. You may find new friends and or a new job. If you need to lose weight, the weight may melt off. When you change, things around you change: for the better. You will fully digest your food, make healthier food selections, and avoid destructive foods. Happily, you will never again revert to old habits.

With every injustice inflicted on others, we attract the same bad energy. We cause our own experiences with few exceptions. We all have an angelic clock, and when it is time to depart, the angels will raise us to the next level—the final destination. With the right choices, this life and the next are so much better. If you are miserable in your heart, you will be unable to gain the real benefits and your choices will be inappropriate. It is time for a major change: you are at the controls.

I have heard some people say I cannot stand all this love and sweetness. Sadly, this means their hearts are closed. They are often intolerant of others, feel cheated, let down, crave attention and never get it. They truly pity themselves, which is the real cause of their downfall. They ask, "Why did this happen to me?" instead of learning the lesson and moving forward. Living in the past and feeding the negative energy of hurt can only result in lower energy levels, as well as physical and mental pain. Those who are so afflicted afflict others. You are the only one who can change your troubled heart so that you can earn a healthier life. All you have to do is love: yourself and God.

May your happy days be so plentiful that you cannot count them. May you learn and grow so quickly that your book of life is filled to the brim. Walk with love in your heart and a song in your soul, because your purpose lives forever.

Judy Kay Gray, M.S., an expert in nutritional science, travels throughout
the world teaching, lecturing, and learning from the world around her.
She is the author of the love story, *The Greatest Treasure of All,* and
the co-author of numerous books. To contact Ms. Gray,
call 1-847-473-4700 or e-mail,
greatesttreasure@hotmail.com.
To purchase books and
tapes: 1-800-243-5242.

Your Gums Could Kill You

By Brian K. Dennis, DDS

What is the most common disease or illness in the world today? No, it is not the common cold or the flu. It is gum disease. The American Dental Association estimates that up to 80 percent of the adult population in the United States has some form of gum disease. Gum disease or periodontal disease, as it is called in the dental profession, is an infection of the tissues, including the gums, bone and ligaments, that support and help hold your teeth in your jaws. Healthy gums are characterized by a pink color, are firm to the touch, have a sharp edge where they meet the teeth, and have a stippled texture such as an orange peel.

Gum or periodontal disease is further separated into two different categories. The first or earliest form of gum disease is gingivitis. Gingivitis could cause your gums to be red, swollen, spongy, and tender. They may bleed easily when brushing or flossing your teeth and give you bad breath, or you may not notice any of these symptoms at all. Gingivitis affects only the gums, not the underlying bone. Gingivitis is caused by plaque, a sticky buildup of proteins, bacteria and food debris which adheres to your teeth. If plaque is not removed regularly the bacteria and their toxic wastes will start an infection in your gums. Also, portions of the plaque can calcify and form a hard substance called calculus or tartar, which is difficult to remove and further irritates your gums. The good news is that gingivitis is reversible. Gingivitis does not affect the bone and can easily be treated. However, if left untreated gingivitis could progress into the next more serious condition of periodontal disease called periodontitis.

There are many different types of periodontitis. The most common forms of the disease are aggressive periodontitis, chronic periodontitis, and periodontitis from a systemic disease such as diabetes. Periodontitis has also been called pyorrhea. Pyorrhea literally means, "pus flowing" which describes the later stages of the disease. Periodontitis has been dubbed the "silent killer of teeth" because it does not hurt. Periodontitis is characterized by bacterial infections in the jawbone. The bacteria and their waste products, combined with your body's immune system fighting the infection actually cause the destruction of the bone and ligaments supporting your teeth. You can have this type of infection for years and never even know that you have periodontitis. You may never notice any of the warnings signs until it is too late. The disease starts with a little or early bone loss and progresses to moderate then advanced bone loss. Your gums will eventually pull away from your teeth. Your teeth may loosen and separate. You could have pockets of pus such as gum abscesses or

www.mentorsmagazine.com

gum boils and chronic bad breath (halitosis). Ultimately this destruction will result in the loss of some or all of your teeth if it is not stopped. As mentioned earlier, gingivitis is reversible but periodontitis is not reversible. Once the bone has been destroyed it is gone forever.

There are a lot of factors which increase the risk of developing periodontal disease, beginning with poor oral hygiene. Smoking and chewing tobacco increases your risk for periodontitis by more than four times. Diseases such as diabetes and osteoporosis increase your chances for gum disease and the loss of teeth. The U.S. Surgeon General's Report on Oral Health states that 95 percent of the people with diabetes also have periodontitis. A recent article in General Dentistry, the journal for the Academy of General Dentistry, describes studies that show a connection between periodontal disease and osteoporosis. Experimental medications for treating osteoporosis may help prevent tooth loss. Obesity may be linked to gum disease. A Case Western Reserve study concluded that obese adults from 18 to 34 years old were 76 percent more likely to have periodontal disease than average weight individuals the same age. Medications such as anti-epileptic drugs, steroids, heart medications, birth control pills, and cancer therapy will cause inflammation of the gums resulting in periodontal problems. Hormonal changes during pregnancy can cause "pregnancy gingivitis" leading to red, swollen, bleeding and painful gums.

Crooked teeth will trap food, making it more difficult to clean the teeth, irritating the gums and allowing infections to start. Grinding or clenching your teeth can put stressful forces on your teeth, gums and bone which increases the rate of destruction of these tissues. Dental restorations such as crowns, bridges, and partial dentures that no longer fit, as well as old, worn-out, broken-down fillings can trap food and bacteria which will cause periodontal disease. Stress is another risk factor for gum disease. The University of New York-Buffalo, the University of North Carolina and the University of Michigan all studied the effects of stress on the oral health of over 1,400 subjects. Those volunteers under more emotional stress were at greater risk for infections in the mouth, inflamed gums, bleeding gums and loss of bone in their jaws.

Now for the scary part. Recent research has linked gum disease to heart disease, strokes, oral cancer, respiratory diseases, and premature, low birth weight babies in pregnant women. The statement that "my gums just bleed a little" can lead to a heart attack. Yes, your gums could kill you! Cardiac surgeons, orthopedic surgeons and dentists have long known that routine dental procedures such as cleanings and extractions can introduce bacteria into the blood stream and cause infections in high risk individuals with certain heart problems and those with recent total joint replacements. In the hit TV show "Extreme Makeover" one patient's breast augmentation surgery was cancelled due to the fact she had periodontitis. This uncontrolled infection could compromise the results of the plastic surgery by infecting the breast implant procedure.

There have been over 200 different kinds of bacteria found in the mouth. It has been said that having periodontal disease is like having an open wound the equivalent of nine square inches! This is a super highway for the bacteria to get into your blood stream and travel around your body to get into major organs and start new infections. New research shows that people with gum disease may be at a higher risk for heart disease than those who smoke, have high cholesterol, or high blood pressure. The current theory is that the bacteria in the mouth enters the blood through the infected gums and are carried to the heart. The bacteria then lodge themselves in the heart and can cause problems such as heart disease and endocarditis (a life threatening infection of the lining of the heart).

Research at the University of North Carolina has found that periodontal disease increases the level of a protein called C-reactive protein or CRP. CRP is produced by the body when there is inflammation present. CRP can easily be identified through a blood test and is also a marker for atherosclerosis. Atherosclerosis causes damage to the walls of major arteries and veins in the body. Bacteria associated with periodontal disease can cause blood clots and fatty plaques to be deposited in these damaged blood vessels, which can block the flow of blood, triggering heart attacks. These deposits can break off, get carried away by the blood stream to the brain and block a blood vessel to cause strokes. Another study published in the New England Journal of Medicine discovered that patients with high levels of CRP are two times more likely to have heart attacks and strokes than those with high cholesterol. The study went on to say "other possible triggers include high blood pressure, smoking and lingering low level infections such as chronic gum disease." The number one cause of death in the United States is heart disease.

If you have gum disease you are more at risk for developing oral cancer. The Centers for Disease Control and Prevention conducted a survey from 1988 to 1994 and found that people with periodontal disease were two times more likely to develop a precancerous lesion and four times more likely to form a tumor in the mouth than those with healthy gums. This is a landmark study because it is the first one to show a link between gum infection and oral cancer. Other studies have linked other types of infections with cancer. For example, the human papilloma virus is associated with cervical cancer and h. pylori bacteria are associated with stomach cancer. Data shows that incidence of oral cancer is increasing. In women, oral cancer has increased from 15 percent to 33 percent over the last 45 years. Tongue cancer in the male population under 40 has been increasing. Early detection of oral cancer is the key to treatment. If detected late, the five year cancer survival rate is only 50 percent.

More new research associates periodontal diseases with respiratory diseases, such as pneumonia, and chronic obstructive pulmonary diseases, such as chronic bronchitis and emphysema. Chronic obstructive pulmonary diseases affect about 15 million people and are the fourth leading cause of death in the

United States. There are several theories about how the gum diseases are linked to respiratory diseases. Poor oral hygiene leads to increased numbers and the types of harmful bacteria in the mouth. As the bacteria thrive they cause changes in the oral environment which allow these harmful bacteria to adhere more easily to surfaces in the body such as the throat, airway and lungs. These infectious bacteria are inhaled into the lungs everyday and form a colony in the respiratory system. This may set up an infection in the lungs, such as bacterial pneumonia, or induce the destruction of lung tissue. The people who are most at risk are those who are debilitated, hospitalized or living in long term care facilities and those who have immune system problems.

Research studying pregnant women with gum disease shows that they are more likely to deliver premature low birth weight babies than those with healthy gums. It is well known that premature infants develop more serious and long lasting health problems. Premature delivery is the number one cause of new born infant deaths and the cause of one half of all serious long-term neurological damage in newborn infants. A study reported in the Journal of the American Dental Association concludes that women in their second trimester of pregnancy with periodontal disease increase their chance of delivering prematurely by 4.5 to 7 times. In response to gum infection and inflammation, your body produces prostaglandins to help control inflammation. One theory is that the extra prostaglandins produced in response to gum disease may cause a pregnant women to go into labor too soon, before the baby is fully developed.

Infections in your mouth can affect your entire body. New research is coming in every day, linking unhealthy gums with other diseases. If you want to be healthy and stay healthy, you must have a healthy mouth. You have to keep your mouth immaculately clean, removing plaque several times a day by brushing, flossing and using other oral hygiene products. Regular visits to the dentist are extremely important. It is estimated that only half the population sees a dentist on a regular basis. Only a dentist can properly diagnose gum disease. Your dentist should customize a recare schedule that best fits you and your mouth. This is determined by the condition of your mouth and your ability to keep it clean. You may need to be seen every six, four, three, or even every month to keep your mouth healthy. You might need to seek treatment from a periodontist – a specialist who only treats periodontal disease. So don't wait, seek out a dentist immediately. It could mean your life!

Dr. Brian Dennis practices preventive, cosmetic and esthetic restorative dentistry in Albuquerque, New Mexico. He lectures nationally, and is a member of both the American Academy of Cosmetic Dentistry and Academy of General Dentistry. For more information, visit www.dennistry.com or e-mail him at bdennis33@msn.com.

Natural Highs:
Boost Your Energy – Naturally!

By Hyla Cass, M.D.

You may feel less energetic than you used to – running out of steam part way through the day, or having trouble getting up in the morning. You may chalk it up to "just getting older," but most energy-related health issues are unrelated to age. The truth is, we are living in a world that never sleeps.

Everything from supermarkets to TV and the Internet are available 24/7. Many of us are trying to keep impossible schedules as we juggle work, home and family responsibilities. We may give up an hour or two of sleep just to try to stay on top of our busy lives. The fact is, without adequate sleep – anywhere from 7-9 hours a night – we lose in both efficiency and overall health. There is also the Standard American Diet (well-named "SAD" for short), full of nutrition-deficient refined foods that are simply not able to sustain us properly.

The Stimulant Roller Coaster

We may turn to unhealthy stimulants like sugar, caffeine, nicotine, alcohol (which acts first as a stimulant), and even drugs, legal and otherwise to give us a boost. These substances make us feel good by triggering the emotional center of the brain, called the *limbic system*, to release *dopamine*, the pleasure molecule.

So far so good. But there is no free lunch here. These highs evaporate all too quickly, often leaving us to cope with a nasty aftermath – mood swings, emotional depletion, physical exhaustion, and even addiction. We feel even worse than before we started. It's not simply that the positive effect wears off, but we now have to cope with a reaction called *down-regulation*. Nature's way of maintaining balance is by quickly shutting down some receptors in the brain, thereby dampening the effects of the excessive dopamine release. As a result, we need more of the stimulant, more frequently, to get the same good feelings and high energy that we did initially.

At the same time, in response to the stimulants, your stress glands, the adrenals, go into hyperdrive. They ultimately become exhausted and no longer able to respond – and neither are you. So, turning to stimulants to rev up your engine will only further deplete an already bankrupt system.

Mentor
#7

On top of this, our very own stress hormones, adrenaline and cortisol, act like stimulants in that they promote the release of dopamine. While this is Mother Nature's way of helping us deal with pain, it can also lead to an addiction to stress itself! Ever think of yourself as a "stress junkie," finding it hard to chill on a weekend or while on vacation? Most of us are: we have become hooked on our own inner chemicals!

The Truth about Stimulants

Caffeine – Caffeine is what gives coffee, tea, and other beverages their "kick." But caffeine is addictive and packs some heavy withdrawal symptoms (fatigue, headache, and irritability, to name a few). Also, because it overstimulates your nervous system, caffeine can cause a rapid or irregular heartbeat, and increases your risk of high blood pressure and heart attacks.

Refined sugar – Grabbing a sweet snack for a quick pick-me-up taxes your system. Your cells struggle to process an overload of sugar that hits your bloodstream much faster than more complex natural varieties such as those found in fruit. Once the rush is gone, you crash in a low-blood-sugar malaise, and crave more. Your arteries, nerves, kidneys, and eyes can suffer from this sugar roller coaster, and you are at risk for diabetes, an increasing epidemic in our society.

Chocolate – Don't assume it's only the sugar and caffeine in that truffle that's picking you up. Cocoa, the main ingredient, contains some highly addictive stimulants. These can cause you to crave more sugar-and caffeine-filled chocolate, with all the attendant health risks.

Nicotine – A powerful poison, nicotine is proven to be more addictive than heroin. As the primary stimulant in cigarettes, nicotine works in a similar way to caffeine. However, along with this energizing "jolt" comes high risks for cancer and heart disease.

Amphetamines – Prescribed for years as "diet pills," these powerful drugs spawned a generation of "speed" addicts in the 50's and 60's. Aside from the serious withdrawal symptoms, amphetamines raise your heart rate and increase your risk of heart attack.

Our Brain on Natural Highs

This is where my life's work comes in – helping people to regain their energy and enthusiasm for life through the use of the right nutrients. These come from the food we eat – carbohydrates, fats and proteins.

Carbohydrate is converted into glucose (blood sugar) which is burned in the cells as fuel to create energy. It is important to eat complex, fiber-laden carbohydrates that burn slowly instead of refined sugars, which give you a quick sugar high, followed by a crash.

"Good fats" such as those found in fatty fish (salmon, mackerel) or in flax oil help make up the brain cells, which are 70% fat. "Bad fats" such as hydrogenated oils and those found in fried foods will actually interfere with healthy brain cell formation.

Protein, found in eggs, fish, meat, or vegetarian sources such as tofu, is broken down into its component amino acids. With the help of vitamins and minerals, these are then turned into "neurotransmitters" or chemical messengers.

Neurotransmitters

There are hundreds of different neurotransmitters in a healthy body. Most of them are specialized: dopamine and adrenaline increase our energy and alertness, helping us respond to stress. The endorphins make us euphoric. Serotonin is both calming and mood-elevating. Acetylcholine drives our memory. GABA balances and relaxes us.

Traveling across tiny gaps or *synapses* between *neurons* (nerve cells) in our brains and bodies, the neurotransmitters send an electrical message down the line to the next neuron, and so on until the signal reaches the intended destination – perhaps a muscle or nerve. Problems arise when nutritional deficiencies hamper the body's ability to produce the neurotransmitters in sufficient amounts, causing us to feel lethargic and run down.

Even with a fairly good diet, we often need a further energy boost. This may be due to your own genetic make-up, a nutrient-deficient diet, the toxic environment, or simply, the increased demands of daily life. Fortunately there are a number of safe and well-researched supplements – vitamins, minerals, herbs and amino acids – that can do the trick. Unlike other energizing substances that give you only a quick fix to spur your cells into temporary hyperactivity, the right nutrients actually help your body to increase the production of neurotransmitters.

Essential Cofactors: Vitamins and Minerals

A recent headline in the respected *New England Journal of Medicine* recommended that for optimum health and nutrition, besides eating a nutrient-rich diet, you need to take a daily multivitamin.

What is so important about vitamins and minerals? Aside from many other functions, they act as essential co-factors, or chemical helpers, in the production of neurotransmitters. Without their help, the transformation of amino acids

into neurotransmitters could not take place. The family of B vitamins, for example, can protect you against depression, anxiety, stress, fatigue, mental dullness, emotional fragility, and even boost your IQ.

Here is some convincing research on vitamin-power. Ninety students were assigned to one of three groups: one received a multivitamin and mineral supplement; the second, an identical-looking placebo (dummy pill); and the third, nothing. After seven months, the IQ of those taking the supplements had increased by a staggering nine points! An increase of only *five points* would get half the learning disabled children out of special schools and back to normal schooling. These results have been borne out in a preliminary study by The Healthy Foundation (www.healthfound.org), of which I am president.

A high-potency multivitamin and mineral formula should form the basis of your supplement program, supplying adequate amounts of vitamins A, B, C, D, E, and assorted minerals – calcium, magnesium, iron, zinc, manganese, chromium, and other trace minerals. Take additional antioxidant nutrients, especially at least 1000 mg of vitamin C and 400 I.U. of vitamin E. Add some essential fatty acids (1 gram of fish oil or flax oil) to further support brain and hormonal function.

Here are Some Winning Energizers

1. Tyrosine:

If you are feeling tired and slow, have trouble getting out of bed in the morning, and have difficulty concentrating, try the amino acid tyrosine. Producing energizing neurotransmitters like *adrenaline* and *dopamine*, as well as helping to make thyroid hormone, it acts like natural caffeine without the downsides, and also has mood enhancing benefits.

2. Adaptogenic Herbs

Adaptogens are herbs that help the body by supporting the adrenal or "stress-fighting" glands. While Western medicine tends to ignore the adrenal glands, traditional systems such as Chinese medicine (TCM) test for adrenal activity, and rely on adaptogenic herbs to deal with a variety of stresses, including infection, exertion, sleep deprivation, and emotional stress. They seem made-to-order for modern lifestyles!

Here are some adaptogens that research shows can boost energy, mood, memory, and endurance, as well as strengthen the immune system:

a. Siberian Ginseng (*Eleutherococcus sentiscosus*) – By increasing cellular oxygenation while normalizing blood sugar (and blood pressure) levels, this natural stimulant supports the adrenal system – which boosts both physical and mental energy and performance.

b. Reishi mushroom extract (*Ganodermum lucidum*) – By stabilizing adrenal hormones, this side-effect free ancient Chinese secret sharpens thinking while both calming and energizing the entire body. As a fringe benefit, it can also help lower blood pressure.

c. Rhodiola (*R. rosea*) (stimulation, mental sharpness, mood) – Boosting levels of the neurotransmitter *serotonin* in the brain, *rhodiola* has been shown to increase energy and mental acuity, as well as alleviate depression and boost immunity.

3. Coenzyme Q10 (Ubiquinone)

Called "ubiquinone" due to its being so ever present ("ubiquitous"), Coenzyme Q10, or CoQ10 is a potent antioxidant that also helps to convert the nutrients we eat into energy. Being fat-soluble, it should be taken with some fat-containing food, such as peanut butter.

4. Trimethylglycine

Often lacking in the body due to poor nutrition, this naturally occurring substance, crucial for neurotransmitter production, converts *homocysteine* – a substance dangerous to the heart – into an energy enhancer called *dimethylglycine*.

Top Tips for a Natural Energy Boost

Experiment with the above supplements or simply take a formula that combines these ingredients in the correct proportions. One of the best is *Energy Formula*, which is based on the information in my book, *Natural Highs*.

Now that you understand the connection between energy and nutrition, it will be easier to incorporate these principles into your own life. Remember, too, that the neurotransmitters are produced by you, in your own brain, enabling you to enhance the process and produce your very own natural highs. In addition to feeding your brain with the right nutrients, positive thoughts go a long way toward raising your "happy" brain chemicals. Our mind-power is a remarkable and often untapped resource in our search for happiness.

Here are my top 8 tips for sustained energy and positive feelings, and to deal with that end-of-the-day lag:

1. Eat a healthy diet (as described in *Natural Highs* under "Natural Highs Basics.")

2. Take a daily high quality multivitamin/mineral formula.

3. Take supplements that support neurotransmitter production.

4. Get sufficient sleep.

5. Take a bath with essential oils of lemon, eucalyptus, cinnamon, or peppermint dispersed in the water, or scent your room with them.

6. Maximize the light in your room with natural daylight.

7. Do aerobic exercise. Twenty minutes daily will do wonders for your energy level not to mention your mood. Yoga, t'ai chi, or any other form of movement will also add another dimension.

8. Turn on some stimulating music, and dance up a storm.

If it seems like you are always tired, and diet or lifestyle changes don't help, then you should consult your healthcare provider. Look for chronic infection (viral, bacterial, yeast), or hormonal imbalances, including those of the thyroid and adrenal glands. Most conventional physicians will send you home telling you to come back "when you are really sick," so it's best to see one who practices integrative medicine, and looks beneath your symptoms to find the root cause.

In conclusion, there is no need to surrender to the blaahs. Give your body the opportunity to rejuvenate itself with natural energy-enhancing products and activities, and you will be off and running. Feeling alive and alert, you'll not only get more done but you'll have more fun doing it.

Based on my book, *Natural Highs: Supplements, Nutrition, and Mind/Body Techniques to Feel Good All the Time*. For more information read the book, and/or visit my website at www.cassMD.com.

Hyla Cass, M.D., is a noted author, speaker, consultant, and media expert in the areas of nutritional medicine and psychiatry, which she combines in her clinical practice. She serves as President of the Healthy Foundation (www.healthfound.org), which provides daily nutritional supplements to at-risk children nationwide. An assistant clinical professor of psychiatry at UCLA School of Medicine, Dr. Cass is also author of several books, most recently, *Natural Highs: Supplements, Nutrition and Mind-Body Techniques to Feel Good All the Time* and *The Yeast Connection and Women's Health*.
For more information including supplement recommendations,
visit www.cassMD.com.

The Mystery of Water

By Josef Tyls, MSc, Ph.D., Ind. Eng

"Water carries embedded energy patterns that seem to correspond to life-affirming and life-challenging energies that are now visible for the first time."

Water was once considered the most sacred of elements. The foundation upon which all civilizations are built is tied directly to the presence of water. The foundations of religions, stories and myths can also be traced back to life-giving and ever-mysterious water. The focus given to the role of water in living systems is receiving public attention like no other time in recent history.

Water is the Lens for the Formative Process of Life

In recent studies, Dr. Masaru Emoto of Yokohama Municipal University in Japan has shown that water carries embedded energy patterns that seem to correspond to life-affirming and life-challenging energies that are now visible for the first time. The technique developed by Dr. Emoto allows one to see the internal structure of water unfolded as a form or pattern. The frozen water droplet picture of industrially polluted water reveals a chaotic structure of damaged water (deconstructed, inhibited, annihilated - the area is void of form), while unspoiled spring water displayed the harmonics of coherent nesting waveforms (the rosetta patterning the display of form is present).

What is Oxygenated Water?

Oxygenated and oxygen-enriched water is a relatively new idea in the marketplace, in which water is specially treated using unique proprietary methods to enhance the level of saturated oxygen. In recent years a few bottled water companies have developed systems to enrich the levels of oxygen in their water products so as to increase their water quality. Re-oxygenated water clearly shows very good structural patterning, effectively bringing damaged water back to the vitality of uncontaminated spring water. The enrichment processes that create oxygenated water are similar to the way extra amounts of carbon dioxide are saturated into water to create soft drinks.

Extra oxygen offers several benefits, mainly related to the oxygen being conveyed directly to the body through absorption upon consumption. Water

www.mentorsmagazine.com

essentially hydrates the body, especially when exercising or playing sports. Oxygen-enriched water, compared to filtered water, greatly reduces lactic acidosis (internal muscle burn) and enhances overall performance output, allowing longer aerobic workouts and faster recovery times. With higher levels of oxygen in the blood from the oxygen-enhanced water, all biological waste and by-products from body functions are easily reduced through oxidation. This effectively deactivates potentially toxic substances and allows for faster and safer elimination cycles via skin and urine.

Oxygen has been also shown to enhance immune functions, which can be a major benefit for many health-related conditions. In addition, reducing toxic buildup has long-term beneficial effect because toxicity is generally the cause of most degenerative diseases.

The overall effect on the body is one of enhancing all body functions, reducing toxic buildups and enhancing waste elimination, thereby promoting good general health.

Health and Cellular Mortality

Otto Warburg, the director of the Max Planck-Institute for cell physiology in Berlin-Dahlem received the Nobel Prize on June 30, 1966 for research on cancer and its cause. In his address at Lindau, Lake Constance, Germany, Mr. Warburg stated that **the primary cause of cancer is hypoxia.** Hypoxia is the state in which oxygen in the ambient media (being blood and lymphatic fluids) and/or within the cell and tissue, is suppressed by a number of **toxin interactions**, which interfere with oxygen transport and respiration.

Once the environment is predominantly anaerobic (oxygen deprived), the aerobic microbiological systems mutate forward fermentation in order to survive. The resulting fermentation creates alcohol-type by-products and effluents (*Fundamentals of microbiology*, Frobisher, by WB Saunders Comp. 1957). The state of fermentation is toxic to all aerobic and multi-celled organisms, therefore causing mutations to develop.

An anaerobic chain reaction is then evident and inevitable once these saturated effluent levels raise beyond the ability of the elimination systems, giving rise to Toxemia, or internal pollution, therefore further creating the condition of hypoxia (*Microbiology*, Michael J. Pelczar, Dr. Roger D. Reid, 1958).

Water and its Relationship to our Health and Wellness

Many studies concerning hydration clearly establish that water is absolutely essential for all proper body functions, including skin and organ integrity, immune system balance, cellular respiration and repair, waste elimination and overall body longevity. An estimated 75% of North Americans are chronically dehydrated, failing to drink the minimum eight glasses of water per day recommended by health and nutrition experts. Not good, considering water is the second most important nutrient to the human body next to oxygen. The body is made up of about 70% water, which plays a vital role in nearly every bodily process: proper digestion and circulation, numerous chemical reactions, nutrient absorption, waste elimination and flexibility of the blood vessels. It regulates body temperature and benefits the skin by acting as an internal moisturizer, as well as preventing premature aging due to toxic buildup.

Many people believe all liquids supply adequate hydration. Not true! Some beverages dehydrate because of their caffeine and sugar content. Caffeine has a diuretic effect on the body, making you urinate more frequently than you need to, which is counter-productive to proper hydration. Drinks such as coffee, milk and juice all require water from the body to be properly digested. Alcohol and some medications can lead to increased fluid loss as well.

In the end, there is no substitute for water in providing the body what it needs for optimal cellular function. When people are ill, eating or drinking anything is probably the farthest thing from their minds. Yet it's vital to maintain a good level of hydration in order to help the immune system fight off infection and assist in eliminating by-products of any illness. Dehydration weakens the body's overall immune system and leads to chemical, nutritional and pH imbalances, which can eventually cause sickness and premature aging. Many ailments classified as "diseases" respond well to proper hydration, including all conditions associated with diabetes, hypertension, high cholesterol, obesity and cardiovascular problems. Asthma can be the body's manifestation of dehydration, and can be prevented or controlled in many cases by simply getting enough water.

How Much?

Individual needs vary depending on factors such as climate, diet and exercise level, but an adequate amount of water is about 10 to 12 full glasses per day. Here's an ideal way to calculate: divide your body weight in half, then drink that amount in ounces (one ounce equals two tablespoons or 30 milliliters). Remember that although you may not need the full amount, drinking water adds no calories to your diet and can be great for your health.

We lose about three liters of water each day through perspiration, urine and respiration, which is why your body's stores must be continually replenished. Waiting until thirst hits isn't the best idea; you're already dehydrated by then! A good gauge to see if you are drinking enough water is your urine. Unless you take B vitamins, your urine should be very pale yellow to almost clear. If it's dark in color (and not because of excess vitamins), then increase your water intake.

If you're one of those geared up to start a workout program this season, getting enough water should be an important concern. It's well known that in hot weather, athletes who don't stay hydrated can suffer from heat cramps, heat exhaustion and heat strokes. But contrary to myth, dehydration can occur at any time of the year. The dryness that occurs during winter can dehydrate the body just as quickly as hot summer conditions. If you have ever experienced extreme tiredness, dizziness or poor coordination while exercising, this was probably due to dehydration. The simple solution is to drink more water before and during all exercise activities. Of course, the easiest way to avoid dehydration at any time is to drink lots of water each day.

Water's Memory

Only pure, primordial, unused water retains the memory of nature and the essence of life. It is a living, vibrant substance that carries the resonant field of our planet and reminds us what 'normal' and 'center' are.

Our cells align to grid lines generated by overlapping 'normal' electromagnetic fields generated by our bodies (Fritz Popp, Ph.D., Germany). Illness is said to be caused by an aberration of these grid lines when our cells go out of alignment and become dysfunctional. These grid lines can be disturbed by any unnatural radiation, geopathic radiations, acid base balance disturbances in our bodies, and pollution. Modern water is not only polluted with physical microbes, heavy metals, radioactive isotopes, chemicals, pharmaceutical drugs, and electronic 'noise,' but also their memory.

Water has a physical memory, called the hydration envelope: when water molecules mix with other molecules, the pattern of their interaction is retained in the water even after the different molecules are gone. This pattern communicates the impact of the different molecules to our system, and this event is the foundation for Homeopathy. Furthermore, when water contains certain combinations of ionic colloidal minerals it becomes conductive as well as capable of remembering a frequency and field.

In a city, millions of telephone lines and electrical systems are grounded into the cold water pipes, which all interconnect. As the water travels through those pipes it is being homeopathically embedded with that chaos – the simultaneous noise of millions of phone calls, faxes, and computers. Then you drink it. Or bathe in it. You get a dose of chaos.

Industrial filtration systems destroy life-affirming subtle energy structures and create chaos at the sub-molecular level leaving the water in a devoid state. This evidence is clearly shown in Dr. Emoto's frozen water droplet photos. www.enews3.com/water

Organic Filtration

The Earth's biosphere ecosystem is based on a closed loop, self-sustaining, perpetual, light-driven mechanism that operates on the photonic power of sunlight. Sunlight causes the waters of the oceans to evaporate and create clouds, which in turn precipitate rain. It is the power of sunlight that creates ozone from oxygen, which gives nature its power to clean organic waste from the air we breathe and the water we drink. The natural media of Earth's soil and rocks filter and mineralize the water creating imbedded harmonics of subtle crystal energy. Granite, Quartz, Zeolites, and Anthracite are just a few of the minerals that affect the quality of natural water. Finally the Flora and Fauna are also an integral part of this well-balanced and important ecosystem in maintaining the living energies that are contained in the waters of the Earth.

Natural Aquifers and Healing Springs

Karlovy Vary in the Czech Republic, Lourdes in France, Baden Baden in Germany, and Halcyon Hot Springs in British Columbia, and Edson, Alberta are all known for their healing qualities. Some of these spring waters have been bottled and sold as health tonics for nearly 150 years. The unique latent energies and therapeutic quality of these waters have been witnessed in Europe for centuries. European mineral water spas are managed by medical communities, which monitor patient progress and see many positive results. The healing effects that take place are the results of enhanced biological processes of the body, through deep tissue osmosis of trace minerals, salts and latent energies. The waters from many of these springs have been tested and found to contain a variety of unique mineral combinations that integrate well with human biology. In the book "Message in the Water" (www.hado.net/message1.html), Dr. Emoto has cataloged frozen water crystal pictures from healing water springs around the world.

The Simple Solution

Water found in its natural state from clean flowing springs and streams that have not been contaminated by industrial waste are the best sources of water. These natural waters contain the proper amount of trace elements, oxygen and subtle energies, which are known to provide the fundamental structures that support all life functions and maintain good health. This organic water system has been perfected over 10 million years and is the finest source of water, which we must insure, maintain and preserve if we are to heal the Earth and ourselves.

Rocky Mountain Spring Water from Edson Alberta, Canada

From high atop the Canadian Rocky Mountains, O'Canada living spring water percolates down through ancient coal seams, which results in a natural carbon filtration process and one of the purest and best tasting waters available on earth. This premium water (with total dissolved solids between 10 - 25 parts per million) is then "Superoxygenated" using a patented diffusion system that dissolves pure oxygen into the source water. The diffusion process stabilizes the oxygen content, which is increased by 700%, extends product shelf life and dramatically improves quality and taste.

In my own experiences with oxygen-enriched water and hydrotherapies, which are many, I have witnessed profound changes to the physiology using only water as the modality. Since 1992 I have spoken on health-related issues surrounding water. At the Advance Water Sciences Symposium in Texas in 1996 I spoke about the next evolution of water technologies, centering on decontamination and restructuring water to enhance the healing aspects of it for spa and hyperbaric applications. I use oxygen-enriched water in my daily maintenance routine to provide the most effective anti-aging modality, since toxic waste accumulation is well known to cause cellular stress, which in turn leads to premature aging. I believe the benefits, including the wonderful, light, refreshing taste, are obvious. I truly feel the difference, as do many other people who consume it.

Josef Tyls, MSc, Ph.D. has been on the forefront of technology for over 20 years. He is an international speaker on water, ozone, natural biologics, human structured consciousness and healing sound technologies. He engineered the first *"All Glass Cold Plasma Ozone Generator"* in 1993, the first commercial re-structured *"Living Essence"* water system in 1994 and also developed the first commercial *"Ultra pure, Hyper-oxygenated"* drinking water system in 1997.
For more information see www.tyls.com

For information on O'Canada Springs and 02Canada Superoxygenated water contact:

02 Water Distributors Ltd.
7198 Vantage Way #128
Delta, BC Canada V4G 1K7
Ph: 604-940-3313
www.o2waterdistributors.com

How I was Cured of a Fatal Disease by Natural Medicine

By Dr. Cass Ingram

In the event of illness, the majority of people place their confidence in modern medicine as the only reliable source of help. As a youth, I was of the opposite thinking: I had little confidence in it. People around me relied upon medications and surgery, but they rarely seemed to get well. What's more, it was obvious that modern medicine treated only the symptoms, rather than the cause. My mother's home remedies, perhaps, created this skepticism. She had concoctions for virtually any illness, and most of them appeared to work. The whole family sought her help and advice. This fired my ambition to be a physician in pursuit of scientifically sound alternative therapies. I believed in the physician's oath to help and do no harm, and I still do.

The curriculum in medical school for natural medicine was disappointing, so I studied and researched on my own and reaped the wisdom of the old professors in private sessions. The natural remedies effectively used since childhood; encouraging review of scientific literature and books; and words of wisdom from Dr. Zink, Dr. TePoorten and others provided such a profound treasury of information, I confidently set about as a new doctor to prescribe a wide range of herbal formulas for my patients. It made sense to me that virtually all drugs originated from herbs and other plants, so using the original plant-based compounds should prove effective. However, the results predicted by books and my experience were not always achieved. Thus, my confidence in herbal medicine began to wane. I hadn't yet learned about the differences in the herbs and their quality and potency. Therefore, I mainly focused on preventive health care using diet, nutritional supplements and family counseling.

Learning the Hard Way

In the midst of a busy practice early in my career, a catastrophe struck. In a matter of weeks, I had two sticks from IV needles that had been used on very sick patients. The technician had failed to deposit the used needles in the appropriate container in the lab, and I accidentally "found" them. The two patients were among the sickest I had ever treated and were part of a group with AIDS-like illnesses. In addition to the contaminated needle punctures, I was under monumental stress with a thriving practice and family discontent. The combination was deadly. Being so direly ill, forced me to close my practice. I lost everything, including my family. For over five years I was unable to work. I experimented with a wide range of herbal medicines and nutritional supplements. None of them worked and nothing relieved the agony in my

                                    www.mentorsmagazine.com

body and soul. With body temperature dropping and all hope dwindling, I was preparing to go to God.

During this time of despair and physical debilitation, dear friends blessed me with support, constant prayers, love and endless care. They provided a home and assistance, since there was no money for food, rent, clothing and the barest of necessities. During this seemingly endless ordeal another close friend, who I had treated and helped with her health problems, made a suggestion. The herb she mentioned seemed almost silly, but there was nothing to lose at that point. In tablet form it caused severe digestive upset, but I actually felt a bit stronger for the first time in years. This was the beginning of a revolution which is now helping millions of people.

There was a need for a more well-tolerated form of wild oregano that could be taken in large quantities. I began experimenting and discovered a safe type of wild oregano oil extracted from the mountain grown spice (P73). I also discovered an herbal form of wild oregano, totally unprocessed and highly potent. By taking these products, my dangerously low body temperature began normalizing and I slowly began gaining strength.

The Process of Trial and Error

Finding an edible oil of oregano was not easy. Research showed that of 80 species of oregano and marjorams, only 4 were truly edible. My associate and I soon discovered we were working with something that felt like liquid fire. It was not particularly user-friendly. As a result of such a low body temperature, my spine would lock and seize. But the excruciating pain and the aggravation was so incredible that I was willing to do anything. So, I became the test animal. The raw oil was applied to the seized spine. It helped, temporarily stopping the pain; but it left a fiery red streak that was sore and the skin peeled. Then an entire vial of the oil was accidentally dropped on my sick bed. Since the cost of the oil was so great, it just couldn't be wasted. The saturated sheet was wrapped around my body for about 10 minutes and then I was rubbed down with a dry wash cloth. This cocooning technique and rubbing caused my body to release a black sooty substance from every pore. This serendipitous treatment helped me to feel better for weeks, and set the stage for further research.

After extensive research and experimentation, regarding the various types of wild oregano, a detailed chemical analysis was obtained. I began to understand the reason that some herbal formulas worked and some failed to work. It is the chemical profile and *where plants grow* that is so important. Thus, the species, soil, and environment play an enormous role in herbal potency. Yet there is, another critical factor: wild versus farm-raised. The wild plant is the only one proven to be effective, plus, it is far safer than the farm-raised varieties.

Further reading revealed ancient uses. A few of the examples include the Babylonians, who used this plant for heart disease, chest disorders, and tuberculosis. The ancient Greeks applied it to wounds, including venomous bites. They too used it for a cardiac tonic. The Romans consumed it as a vitality potion and for lung conditions, and it can still be found in the ruins of a pharmacy in Ephesus today. The Bible mentions it as the purging herb, and Moses used it to fight plague and pestilence.

All the research and reading was encouraging, but it was evident that something had to be done to make the blend more tolerable for extended use. It was helping me so much, but only minute doses could be used. An endless array of unrefined food grade oils were emulsified with the essential oil blend and, finally, the finest extra virgin olive oil, with its own beneficial and protective properties, was the most effective and user friendly. Then, special formulas were developed using the extra virgin olive oil and a blend of this wild essential oil. We found this unique emulsion far superior both topically and internally in comparison to the raw oil. During the research, two levels of efficacy were established. One level was regular strength for daily usage that most everyone could tolerate, and the other was the maximum strength for chronic or severe problems like I experienced. We discovered the combination of internal and topical usage was the most beneficial. Then, in 1995 I mentioned this powerful and blessed substance and how it saved my life with the late Dr. Robert C. Atkins on radio. Little did we realize that because of a terrible, debilitating illness a discovery was made that would help millions.

Since that time modern research has had amazing results with the wild plants and combinations of compatible plants. The scientist assigned the number, P73, to this wondrous blend of proprietary essential oils that brought me back to life. Georgetown University determined that infections by dangerous pathogens, including Candida albicans and drug-resistant staph, could be reversed. Then researchers at Microbiotesting Labs conducted tests that obliterated cold and flu viruses, including the human corona virus. Other research has shown it kills the hepatitis and herpes viruses. It is no wonder that I improved so quickly and dramatically.

The Blessings of Illness

Every event in our lives can increase our understanding and expand our thinking if we allow it to happen. I firmly believed that after 22 years of schooling I would always be a doctor with a busy practice seeing patients every day with no thought of any other endeavor. Yet, all this came to a sudden unexpected stop at age 32. What seemed like the end of my world was actually the beginning. It certainly didn't seem so at the time, and it took years to realize the value of such a painful experience. Then, I realized that instead of seeing people one at a time, day after day, I was released from such a confined destiny to reach out to millions with messages of hope and the option of solutions when others have not dared to offer any. I learned that my illness brought about a discovery so great that it can benefit every living soul. Illness is an opportunity to slow down and seek answers. My path and focus changed for the better. The events that build and strengthen our souls are always intertwined with others. We are never alone, even though it may seem so during the most trying times. My illness was needed. I had to be sick to do the research that led to the cure.

Part of my growth was to understand people better and to learn what role illness plays. Illness is more than an affliction caused by nearly invisible agents, such as bacteria, viruses and fungus, which lie in wait to attack us. They live in every human, but some people succumb and others do not. As I reflected on my own nearly fatal condition it became so obvious the contaminated needles didn't activate it. They were just the end result. The stage had already been set for a break down of my whole life. Yet, the change that resulted is still making a dramatic difference for so many lives. This was obviously the direction that I was meant to go.

God gave us plant medicines to use during those weakened times when illness brings us to a halt. Illness proved to me that those healing plants in the purest forms are powerful healing agents. As a young physician, I learned to disregard and ignore the herbs that books and colleagues so highly recommended. Then, out of necessity I was forced to take a second look, experiment and discover their secrets and how to properly use them. As with everything worthwhile in life, integrity and excellence is part of the power. Now I know what works for those who are suffering.

I have seen patients with a wide range of diseases grow stronger, and many of them even achieve a complete cure. They rid themselves of diseases such as arthritis, diabetes, obesity, chronic fatigue, thyroid disorders, pneumonia, acne, ringworm, psoriasis, asthma, bronchitis, sinusitis, hepatitis, fibromialgia, multiple sclerosis, cardiovascular disease and even cancer. Many people suffer from symptoms such as depression, anxiety, insomnia, itching, headaches, hot flashes, panic attacks, ear aches, aches and pains, incontinence, constipation, diarrhea, heartburn, bloating, still joints and more. Through the natural approach, virtually all of it is reversed. Once a person focuses on getting well, the healing process begins. It may require a multitude of approaches to achieve the results, but by making the decision to get well – that it is okay to be well – the biggest step has been taken. There were times when I wanted to die with a body full of sickness, a broken family and no financial means. Love makes the difference. Those who cared for me refused to give up. That helped me to focus on health and living instead of sickness and dying.

The powers of God have convinced me that regardless of the disease, there is hope for everyone. If the right approach is taken, any disease can be conquered. Think of disease as being in the past. Refuse to cling to it in any way. Never give up hope, and always prepare your soul for the future.

Dr. Cass Ingram is a nutritional physician, expert on natural ways to fight infections, medical researcher, authority on natural medicines and author of more than a dozen books including, *The Cure is in the Cupboard* and *Lifesaving Cures*. His latest books are *Eat Right and Live Longer*, and *The Respiratory Solution*. www.droregano.com

Beyond Dieting
Hormones That Keep Us Fat

By Lorna R. Vanderhaeghe

North Americans are obsessed with their weight. According to the U.S. Federal Trade Commission, more than $36 billion is spent annually in the U.S. on weight loss products and pills. Although we are spending increasing amounts of money to lose weight, we are more overweight than ever. While poor nutrition, specifically intake of dietary fat, bears most of the blame for the surge in overweight individuals, we know that our expanding girth is associated with many factors. Fad products and diets don't work – they lead to binge eating, repeated cycles of weight gain and loss, and are emotionally and physically destructive due to their restrictive nature; in short, they are harmful to your health.

Obesity constitutes the second leading cause of preventable death after smoking and is considered to be the most common nutritional disorder in the industrialized world today. More than 60 percent of the entire U.S. population has a weight problem. The picture is much the same in Canada with data provided by the Canadian Community Health Survey between 1990 and 2001 showing that 48 percent of the Canadian population is packing too much poundage, with 15 percent classified as obese.

Long term studies show that one- to two-thirds of weight lost through dieting is regained within one year and almost all weight is regained within five years. Now you are wondering, "Why bother trying?" Fat loss is not about dieting. It is about eating for a long healthy life. Diets are only considered a success if weight loss is maintained and you have gained energy and vitality in the process. They should satisfy all nutritional needs, be delicious, meet individual tastes and habits, minimize hunger and boost energy.

Fat Children

For children the statistics are most frightening. According to the National Longitudinal Survey of Children and Youth, over one third of Canadian children aged 2 to 11 are overweight and of those, half are obese. More boys than girls were found to be overweight. Preschoolers fared the worst with one in four children between the ages of two and five obese. Statistics are similar in the U.S. Report on America's Children prepared by the National Institutes of Health and the U.S. Census Bureau. That is a lot of fat toddlers, and they are not the ones buying the groceries or driving to fast food restaurants. We must change the way we feed our children. Aside from the health issues associated with being an overweight child, the emotional issues are quite damaging. We

know that overweight children are treated differently by teachers and classmates, causing self-esteem issues which further exacerbate the psychological aspects of eating.

Pharmaceutical companies are pumping billions of dollars into new weight loss drugs to fight the war against fat. Geneticists try to unlock and manipulate the genes that make us fat, hoping for a vaccine that will keep us thin. Yet the secret may be more complicated than reducing calories and exercising more often: our hormones may be contributing to our fatness.

Six Factors That Make Us Fat

Old theories about weight loss were based on the calories in, calories out rhetoric. Simply put, if you ate less food and exercised more, weight loss would occur. Those that exercise daily, eat salad and carrot sticks, drink glass after glass of water and still don't lose weight can vouch that weight loss is not that simple. And we all know the person who can eat whatever they wish, never set foot on a treadmill and never put on a pound. There is a complex interplay of hormonal, biochemical, genetic, physical and lifestyle factors causing our battle of the bulge.

Basal Metabolic Rate

Metabolism is the chemical reactions that take place inside our cells to create energy. All the fuel, including carbohydrates, fats, essential fats, and proteins in the food we eat are broken down to produce the energy the body needs to maintain our body temperature, help us breathe, move our muscles and more. Your Basal Metabolic Rate (BMR) is the rate at which your body burns calories when you are at rest. Thyroid hormones and how much you exercise are two factors, among many, that have an affect on your metabolic rate. A peak operating metabolism can burn up a lot of fuel (food) and create plenty of energy, or conversely a slow metabolism will store the fuel as fat.

To rev up your fat burning furnace eat protein for breakfast, which is known to increase metabolism by 25 percent. That increase lasts for several hours. Use safe thermogenic nutrients including cayenne and bitter orange. Have your thyroid checked.

Liver Function

If you have been dieting for years and were never told a healthy liver is essential for fat loss, it isn't any wonder you may not have reached your goals. The liver is the most important organ in the body, filtering blood, processing and packaging hormones, removing toxins, metabolizing proteins and carbohydrates into energy, manufacturing cholesterol and breaking down fats among hundreds of other vital functions.

Fatty Liver

Excess weight around the middle, whites of the eyes that are dotted with fatty yellow bumps, fatty cysts and skin mottled with 'age spots' are all signs of a congested liver, more commonly called a 'fatty liver.' Clogged bile ducts, inadequate secretion of bile, not enough bile, or an overwhelmed or congested liver from too many prescription drugs, toxins or alcohol can all contribute to a fatty liver. These factors cause our liver to inadequately break down or emulsify fats and our fat cells to store too much fat, promoting weight gain or resistance to fat loss. Bombarded with hundreds of toxins daily from the food we eat and drink, the air we breathe, and the internal chemicals produced as a by-product of daily cellular processes, the liver has a non-stop job of detoxification.

Estrogen Belly

Any disruption of the liver detoxification pathway contributes to excesses or imbalances in hormones, toxins and our ability to lose weight. The liver is responsible for conjugating or combining estrogens and other steroid hormones, certain drugs and chemical compounds. A decreased rate of estrogen excretion via liver detoxification contributes to what we commonly call "estrogen belly," which is simply too much fat around the middle. Too much estrogen, also called estrogen dominance, is one reason why women have a difficult time losing fat around the abdominal area. It is also the reason why men tend to develop a "beer belly" and breasts in their forties and beyond. Too much fat on our body increases our estrogen levels, as fat cells are a storage site for estrogen. Fat cells also manufacture estrogen. This sets up a vicious cycle of too many fat cells manufacturing and storing too much estrogen, which creates high levels of estrogen, which maintains our increased fat.

To correct estrogen metabolism in the liver and our fat cells, we should include the following nutrients in our fat loss program: indole-3-carbinol 150mg, calcium D-glucarate 150mg, curcumin 50mg, Milk thistle 50mg and sulphoraphane 100mcg.

The Fat Storage Hormone

Insulin, a hormone secreted by the pancreas, may be the main culprit contributing to our fatness. The standard excessively high carbohydrate, low protein diet is disrupting our body's ability to regulate blood sugar adequately. When we have too much insulin being pumped out, trying to reduce abnormally high blood sugar, we inevitably gain weight. Our cells become very resistant to insulin and fat loss. Everyone who is overweight has insulin resistance, which puts us at higher risk of heart disease, cancers and diabetes.

Another deadly aspect of high insulin is that it increases the secretion of cortisol, our stress hormone. High cortisol causes a corresponding drop in the hormone dehydroepiandrosterone (DHEA). DHEA helps to increase muscle mass, improve immune function, is a precursor to other hormones and has been called our anti-aging hormone. Most importantly for fat loss, we know that more muscle mass causes increased fat burning and a reduction in insulin. As we can see, high insulin promotes a very negative cascade of effects.

Keep insulin levels normal by eating small protein-rich meals throughout the day and eliminate the white foods (white sugar, white flour, white rice, white pasta, white potatoes).

Leptin, a hormone produced by body fat, is critical in telling the body when to eat and when we are satisfied. We know that in some people the message of satiety is not heard and the fat cells send out more and more leptin, which causes resistance to leptin, increased food cravings and the desire to continue eating. In other people leptin levels are low due to zinc deficiency. Providing 30-60 mg of zinc per day can increase leptin levels, correcting the message to the brain and halting our hunger pangs.

The Cortisol Connection

Unrelenting chronic stress is another factor that promotes weight gain. New research performed at Laval University in Quebec shows chronic stress causes our fat cells to become resistant to fat loss, especially around our abdomen. Cortisol activates fat cells – all fat cells – to store fat! But those that are called central fat cells, found mainly deep in the abdominal wall, have four times the cortisol receptors on their cell membranes. Each time you are stressed, the cortisol-fat mechanism turns on and your body stores more fat to handle all the stress. You learned earlier that cortisol is also increased in response to high insulin levels, so we are getting it from all angles.

Most of us contend with stress on a daily basis due to our fast-paced lifestyle. Stress has now surpassed the common cold as the most prevalent health problem in North America. If we desire weight loss our cortisol levels, through stress management, must be controlled.

Serotonin, a neurotransmitter in the brain made from the amino acids found in proteins, is also involved in notifying your brain that you can put down your fork. Neurotransmitters are messengers that communicate between cells. Low serotonin causes depression, obesity, lethargy, and a preference for refined carbohydrates and overeating because the brain senses it is starving. Those that are hyper-secretors of cortisol exhibit suppressed serotonin levels, which may lead to problems managing weight. We know that in vulnerable persons, depression promotes weight gain. When we diet and restrict protein-rich calories, our serotonin levels also plummet. The connection between serotonin-cortisol and weight gain is currently being heavily researched. Significant impact is made by simply lowering cortisol levels through stress management and the use of specific serotonin-enhancing nutritional supplements including 5-HTP (5-hydroxytryptophan) 50-100mg three times per day.

Food Glorious Food

We put more thought into the fuel we put into our car than we do the food that fuels the body. Quantity of food is given most of the credit for our weight woes when the quality of the food we eat plays an equally important role. Saturated fats, trans-fats, fake fats, aspartame and other artificial sweeteners, refined carbohydrates, processed meats and cheese, diet foods and sodas conspire to make us fat and disrupt our hormones. We would not put polluted oil or gasoline into our car. Yet we fill up our amazing body each and every day with chemically-altered, toxic foods.

Allergies and sensitivities to food also contribute to increased bloating, poor digestion, weight gain, water retention and an overall puffy appearance. Leaky gut syndrome is caused by years of food allergies, bacterial overgrowth in the gut, Candida and stress (high cortisol). The name 'leaky' gut means waste, bacteria, and partially digested food are allowed to pass into the bloodstream. The foreign substances that should have stayed in our digestive system are now floating in the bloodstream, causing additional stress on the liver and fluid retention with some individuals packing around 10 to 15 pound of extra fluids. Our body is approximately two-thirds water, found in all our cells and tissues where it is essential for all bodily functions. But when water becomes trapped in tissues and around cells, detoxification and proper cell function, including the movement of fat into and out of cells, is inhibited.

Too Tired to Move

You know you have to exercise but you have no get up and go. Low thyroid and exhausted adrenals are two reasons why we have no desire to work out. Low thyroid, called hypothyroidism, affects approximately 30 percent of the population. The percentage is higher in the northern hemisphere where sunlight exposure is shorter and therefore vitamin D (used by the body to make thyroid hormone) deficiency is more common. Low thyroid makes you too tired to move. The thyroid gland sets your body's metabolic rate and intimately interacts with your adrenal glands (the glands that sit above your kidneys). If inadequate thyroid hormone is available, the adrenals will be affected and if the adrenals are exhausted, the thyroid is compromised.

The adrenal glands release sex hormones and stress response hormones involved in our body's response to stressors. Long-term elevations of cortisol can exhaust or wear out our adrenal glands. When our adrenal glands become impaired, cortisol levels rise and stay high. Ashwagandha has been researched to show it increases T4 thyroid hormone and supports exhausted adrenals. Include 200 mg per day in your diet.

What Have We Learned?

By now you see the connection between all our hormones, stress, the foods we choose and how they can contribute to weight gain and conversely weight loss. If you have been struggling with your weight, hormone balance may be the reason. The good news is we can maintain a healthy weight by correcting our dysfunctional hormones, reducing stress, eating small protein-rich meals throughout the day to improve insulin utilization, taking a multi-vitamin with minerals containing adequate zinc, adding nutrients to improve liver, thyroid and adrenal function and exercising. In addition, I recommend you look for my new book, *The Body Sense Natural Diet* (Wiley 2004) or visit my website at www.hormonehelp.com.

Lorna Vanderhaeghe is a medical journalist who has been researching and writing on the subject of nutritional medicine for over 20 years. She has a Bachelor of Science degree in Biochemistry and is currently working on completing her Masters in Nutrition. She is an internationally known lecturer who believes in empowering people with health knowledge so they can achieve optimal wellness.

Lorna is the co-author of the award-winning, best-selling book *The Immune System Cure*, now published in six countries and four languages, and author of the Canadian bestseller *Healthy Immunity, Scientifically Proven Natural Treatments for Conditions from A-Z*. She is also the co-author of *No More HRT: Menopause Treat the Cause* and *Healthy Fats for Life*. Her latest book is called *The Body Sense Natural Diet*.
Her website is www.hormonehelp.com

It's Your Attitude...
It's Your Choice

By Tom Bay, Ph.D.

Our attitudes have a major impact on all aspects of our lives – mental, physical, social, financial, spiritual. Our thoughts and beliefs are reflected outwardly to those we come in contact with throughout our daily activities. Most importantly, our attitudes are what form our habits. Good or bad, habits begin with our attitudes.

Habits are learned behaviors that are relatively fixed and hard to change. They occur repeatedly in specific situations. Habits are comfort zone actions or inactions that we learn to do automatically; some are good for us, such as fastening a seat belt, and others aren't, such as overeating or smoking. I'm sure we all have daily no-brainer activities, like opening the newspaper, scanning the headlines, and then going to the sports section, the financials or maybe the comics. We are on automatic pilot at times like these. The same thing can happen with habits – our bodies act while our minds are elsewhere.

Take this concept to the next level. Having a positive attitude, by choice, promotes positive self talk and in turn forms positive habits. A habit of being the best you can be. A habit of wanting to live life and not just exist. Most of the human potential is restricted to a very small circle of our being. We tend to use a very small portion of our resources. In fact, it often takes a crisis or trauma for us to realize our true vital resources and how much greater we are within ourselves. Get in the habit of being the best you can be by using all your abilities – walking your talk and talking your walk.

I think what is really unfortunate is that our attitudes are driven by a world driven by stress. Demands abound to perform at a higher level, to multi-task, to do more in less time in this age of technology. We were told early on that technology would enhance the quality of our lifestyles, giving us less hours in the work week, more personal time, etc. What technology has really done is raise the bar of productivity in the same amount of time.

We all have the same amount of time: 1,440 minutes a day, no **more,** no **less.** But the demands and expectations have dramatically increased. When someone says "fax it" or "email it," when do they expect it? NOW! What did we do before cell phones? We are expected to be available 24-7. When do we realize

MENTOR
#11

69

that the most important person in my life – is **ME.** If I don't take care of myself, then no one is in charge. These are important questions: **Whose** life is it? **Who** is responsible for it? **What** do I plan on doing about it? And most importantly, **When?** If you or I can't take the time to answer these questions then we really are being driven by stress.

I've had more than 7,000 speaking engagements over the past 30 + years, many before pharmaceutical companies. They all agree that most of the top selling drugs in this country are for stress related disorders. This is very understandable when we look at the source of most stress. At about the age of two, we begin to show signs of wanting control of our lives, often referred to as the "terrible twos." This lasts until about three and a half, but surfaces again even more dramatically at about 13 -14 years old and kicks into high gear at 16-17 years.

Our desire for freedom and control surges, becoming a major challenge for our parents. It begins with the desire to drive and own a car – our ticket to independence. Control is the issue. Stress results when we feel out of control of our lives; success results when we control our lives and our destiny, and yet, stress is nothing more than perception. Our attitudes help form our perceptions.

Let me explain in a little more detail. When we meet the "Tigers" in life, regardless of whether they are real or imagined, our bodies prepare to fight or flight. Note that both responses are physical. Our bodies make the appropriate changes to survive:

• Your brain becomes more alert to deal with the situation; if the stress continues, mental exhaustion and headaches occur.

• Due to alarm warnings from your brain, your pituitary gland activates the adrenal glands to start pumping adrenaline and corticosteroids, preparing your body to take physical action.

• Your heart pumps faster and blood pressure rises.

• Your immune system shuts off immediately because it is unnecessary to meet the emergency.

• When you tense up, muscles tighten, arteries constrict, and blood thickens from a consistency of water to molasses in less than three minutes, making your heart pump harder. Your body produces platelets so blood will coagulate quickly if you are wounded.

• Your mouth has a bitter taste.

• Your skin perspires more.

• Your liver sends extra glucose into the bloodstream so you have energy.

• Your body produces four times as much acid in the digestive tract. This makes sure nothing stays there, enabling you to face the tiger without a heavy stomach.

All of these physical changes make you strong in a time of crisis. Here's the kicker: If we continually sweat the small stuff, our bodies remain in a state of vigilance – the blood is a little thicker, the heart beats a little faster, there is more acid in the digestive tract, the immune system is in an off position, etc.

Our attitudes can develop life management habits that are positive and healthy for our desire to **live** life, not just **exist.** Scientists are discovering that disease is not necessarily caused by germs and viruses acting alone. All people have germs but not everyone becomes ill. In addition to hereditary and environmental factors, there is strong evidence that many illnesses are closely linked with the way an individual reacts to life!

Sixteen year-old Melissa Anderson knows how to react to life and injuries. After being struck by a riderless motorcycle, Anderson was rushed to UCI Medical Center in Orange County, California. When doctors removed her ruptured spleen and repaired her damaged liver, they weren't finished. The accident punctured her lung, broke her collarbone and right leg, and caused her brain to swell. Doctors expected Anderson to be hospitalized for months.

When she regained consciousness, Anderson had other plans: she wanted to go home. Twelve days later, she did. "When I want to do something, I just go do it. I worked on getting out of there," she explained. Her doctor, Michael Lekawa, said Anderson's "attitude and willingness to get up and move around despite pain speeded her recovery and prevented side effects such as pneumonia, embolisms, or kidney failure." He added, "The will to recover causes hormonal changes in the body that encourage healing. I absolutely believe that a strong attitude to do well and survive helps you out."

Researchers claim that right attitude is a medicine, and they can back up their claim. Physical and emotional health are interrelated; a person with good emotional health can work, love and play without much internal stress. But things have a way of getting tough, and when they do your emotional health determines your ability to cope. Emotional health is as important as physical health because it helps you visualize, imagine, and anticipate full recovery from illness. Good emotional health should be a goal in life. Hobbies like reading, watching old movies, enjoying nature, gardening, or listening to music can help your emotional health.

In *There's a Lot More to Health Than Not Being Sick,* Bruce Larson writes, "Doctors have been telling me for years that you can't kill a happy man. Then

I press for an explanation and they suggest that unhappiness often precedes illness. Happy people rarely get sick and tend to recover quickly when they do get sick. The unhappy person is a target for any and every kind of illness."

One of my favorite authors and minds of today is Deepak Chopra. Reading all of his material has given me great insight into the mind-body relationship. In *Ageless Body, Timeless Mind* Chopra points out that our bodies eavesdrop on our minds and respond accordingly, which is why it is not a good idea to sigh, "Oh, I'm so fat," "I just can't lose weight," "I never remember names," "I don't do well on tests," "I can't find work," "I never win anything," and on and on... Positive self-talk is critical to establishing a right positive attitude of emotional and physical health. Chopra cited a study by doctors at Tufts University involving adults between 87 and 96 who began a physical fitness program. Some of these frail people needed help just to get out of bed or perform other simple tasks. Eight weeks later their muscles came back "by 300 percent, coordination and balance improved, and an overall sense of active life returned." Chopra noted that by going to the weight-training room, these people showed that they believed in themselves. Despite their infirmities, they had some right attitudes.

I am very blessed. For over thirty years, I have been in the professional speakers business. I've written three books, appeared before all the Fortune 500 companies, and had over 7,000 speaking engagements. I've never had to work a day in the past thirty plus years. My dad was right: "Find something to do that you love and you'll never work again."

The core material in my book and my talks is based on attitude. In fact, the tag line for my company is "It's Your Attitude... It's Your Choice." Little did I know how important this statement would become in my personal life. As I stated previously, I've asked audiences over and over again to answer the following questions: Whose life is it? Who's responsible for it? What do you plan on doing about it? And last question...When?

Six years ago I was diagnosed with prostate cancer and the answers to these questions became much more significant to me. None of the questions could be answered until I recognized what I had control over and what I did not. It seemed so easy from the lecture platform. Now that my life was at risk, thoughts of my family, loved ones, grandkids, my business, etc., etc. were all spinning in my head. Combine these thoughts with the anger of "Why me?" I did all the right things: exercise, diet, rest...the doctor interrupted my thoughts with one very enlightening statement. "Tom, cancer doesn't care." This slapped me back into focus. I had been spending more time on things I had no control over and very little time on what I really controlled. I checked out all the offered solutions, asked lots of questions, and made the decision to have seed implants. I checked into the hospital at 1:30 p.m., had the procedure at 4:00 p.m., and checked out of the hospital at 8:30 p.m. that same day. My attitude had taken control: I did not choose to be a member of this "club," but my reaction was my choice. I had a life to live. Eventually, I was cancer-free.

Two years later, I was given another opportunity to walk my talk. I went to see my doctor for what I thought was a week-long bout with the flu. I walked into his office for my 2 o'clock appointment, looking forward to my blood test results. My doctor followed me into the patient room. He asked five questions in quick succession, to which I answered "yes" in each case. Then the bomb dropped. He told me I had complete renal failure and I must go immediately to the hospital for dialysis of my kidneys. Less than two hours later, I was having the impurities in my system mechanically removed. Two days later, they gave me the news that my kidneys had failed because I had multiple myeloma. "Doc, I don't have time for cancer," I said. "What are we going to do now?" I will never forget his response: "Tom, I like your attitude." Little did I know that prostate cancer was just a test run for my attitude towards myeloma.

I want to live life, not just exist. The more I talk with other cancer patients, the more I am convinced that attitude has a major impact on each and every one of us as we face each day. It starts with the recognition of what events we do and don't control. Reach out, grab the events that you can control and do the best you can to adapt to the ones you don't. You and I are too important not to take control of our destiny, as best we can under the circumstances. We are in a club that none of us chose, with a membership we cannot cancel. Our attitude impacts all we do and affects all those around us. Attitude is the little thing that makes a big difference. Right or wrong, good or bad, positive or negative, It's Your Attitude... It's Your Choice. Make it a great day by making a great choice.

***

Tom Bay, Ph.D., is internationally known as a speaker, author, and executive consultant focusing on attitude as the key to success. He has inspired thousands of individuals to redirect their energy, leading to higher morale and an overall more productive attitude. He is the author of *Look Within or Do Without: 13 Qualities Winners All Share*, and co-author of *Change Your Attitude: Creating Success One Thought at a Time*. For more information, visit www.tombay.com or call 888/440-8000.

Starch Blockers:
An Effective Tool Against the Rising Tide of Obesity

By Steven Rosenblatt, M.D., Ph.D.

America is faced with an epidemic of obesity. This epidemic is increasing daily. Over 61% of the US population is overweight or obese. It is estimated that 25% of our children are overweight. Obesity is the number two preventable health care problem in America, behind smoking. It is estimated that by 2010 it will be number one.

The consequences of this are staggering. The resulting soaring increase in number of diabetics is beginning to strain the already overburdened health care system. The resultant effects of diabetes – neuropathy, nephropathy, vascular disease, and retinopathy – will surely cause our future health care delivery system to collapse.

In trying to treat the root cause of this problem, a number of researchers have proposed the wide-spread introduction of a new ingredient in the fight against obesity. This new substance is a natural extract of a common bean. It is safe and effective even when taken over extended periods of time. This product has been called a starch blocker and was given the generic name of phaseolamine.

The History of Starch Blockers

Starch blockers were first developed under the direction of the legendary Howard Hughes by his group at Howard Hughes Medical Institute. In 1971, Hughes spotted an article in an obscure scientific journal (*Acta Scientifica Venezolane*). For reasons unknown, mice in an experiment that had been conducted in Venezuela had died of starvation, even though they'd been fed a seemingly nutritious diet. The article said that perhaps some form of "anti-nutrient" had caused the baffling starvation.

Hughes assigned a team of researchers at the Miami institute to look into the mystery. Over the next two years, this research team linked the Venezuelan mystery to existing knowledge about certain "anti-nutrient" proteins that inhibit food digestion by binding with the digestive enzymes of insects, animals, and human beings.

It has been known since the 1940s, for example, that raw, unprocessed wheat contains small amounts of a protein that binds with the receptor sites on alpha-amylase, the enzyme that digests starch. This makes the amylase temporarily incapable of breaking down starch. The protein stays in the system for only one or two hours. It's quickly moved through the digestive tract, along with the enzyme and the other food substances that were eaten, and is excreted.

While it is in the system, though, it renders amylase incapable of breaking down the starch molecule. This undigested starch then passes through the system in its fibrous form, with the other foodstuffs. Because the undigested starch stays in whole-molecule form, it does not release any calories. In effect, it becomes an indigestible fiber.

What researchers discovered at the Howard Hughes Medical Institute – and in related research at the University of Miami – was that the plants with the most abundant amounts of this enzyme-inhibiting "anti-nutrient" were white kidney beans. White kidney beans had primarily composed the diet of the Venezuelan mice that had starved to death.

The researchers named the enzyme-inhibiting substance in white kidney beans "phaseolamin." The word is derived from the Latin word for kidney beans, "phaseo vulgaris," combined with "am" (short for "amylase") and "in" (short for "inhibitor"). Phaseolamin is a vegetable glycoprotein with a very specific molecular weight (approximately 450) and is part of a specific plant protein.

The initial interest in phaseolamin among almost all researchers was as a tool to fight diabetes. Researchers were well aware that eating excessive amounts of starch can be critically injurious to people with diabetes, because it spikes the glycemic curve. They hoped phaseolamin would help flatten this curve.

For several years, during the 1970s, they worked on isolating phaseolamin from other substances in kidney beans, especially "lectins," which can cause blood cells to clump together. This refinement process was exceptionally difficult. It was easy to just grind up beans, but that left in too many impurities. Ground-up beans did seem to have a moderate enzyme inhibiting action, but they caused too many side effects, such as bloating and diarrhea.

 In 1982, crude bean extracts began to appear on the market, and were sold for weight loss. Sales of these products were strong, and for several months these crude "starch blockers" became a new fad.

The Food and Drug Administration quickly intervened. They ruled that it wasn't legal for retailers to claim that these starch blockers caused weight loss. To do so would be a health claim, and at that time, the only products that could make health claims were drugs. However, a couple of companies that had adequate refining processes did continue to market them, without any promotion, and they remained moderately popular in a few other countries, including Italy.

Fortunately, research persisted at the Mayo Clinic. Doctors there continued to be fascinated by the potential of starch blockers for helping diabetics. They continued looking for ways to improve the extraction process. Gradually it became clear that they needed to increase the amount of active starch inhibition material in each dosage, and to eliminate all possible contaminants. Finally a pure, much more active product was produced. The new Mayo Clinic formula was more effective, and proved quite capable of inhibiting starch breakdown by human amylase, in test tubes.

Between 1984 and 1999, researchers at the Mayo Clinic completed 12 studies and published all of them in peer reviewed medical journals, including *The New England Journal of Medicine*, *Gastroenterology*, *The Mayo Clinic Proceedings*, *Pancreas*, and *Nutrition*. The Mayo Clinic studies gradually recreated interest in starch blockers among other members of the international biological research community. In the early 1990s, researchers at several major medical institutions in Japan became fascinated by the potential of starch blockers. From 1992 until 2001, 10 separate studies were conducted at Kyushu University, Hokkaido University of Sapporo, Osaka University, and other Japanese universities and medical institutions.

New studies on improved extraction methods proliferated around the world and yet despite this, major problems remained. By the mid-1990s, no institution had developed a refinement process that could deliver a highly potent version of starch blockers to the market at a price that most people could afford.

Finally a group of scientists at Pharmachem Laboratories began to work on an even more refined extraction process. The primary goals were to make a more potent, concentrated formula, and a more stable formula, which would pass intact into the small intestine, where almost all starch digestion occurs. This group was also intent upon finding ways to extract the formula with water, rather to extract it by using solvents, as had the Mayo Clinic. The solvents the Mayo Clinic had used had not been toxic, but Pharmachem had a long history of producing supplement materials without resorting to solvent extraction. They wanted to use only purified water.

By 2000, the Pharmachem research team was satisfied with their formula. What they had produced was so different from the original formulas that it was no longer phaseolamin. However, everyone in the field of biological science was accustomed to the term 'phaseolamin,' so they extrapolated from the common nomenclature and called it "phaseolamin 2250," or "Phase 2."

Phase 2 is markedly stronger than the Mayo Clinic's substance. It is more concentrated, more stable in the gastrointestinal tract, and is completely free of impurities.

The Plan

Starch blockers are an important tool in any weight loss program. They allow some starch and carbohydrates to be brought back into what is a protein based diet. Modern research has shown that a high protein diet is effective at reducing weight and controlling blood sugar levels, but it is very difficult to stay on this type of diet for more than a few weeks. Many people get very agitated and nervous on a carbohydrate restricted diet. In general "denial diets" are very difficult to maintain for extended periods of time.

By using starch blockers with each meal about 75% of the starch calories can be prevented from entering the system. One gram of starch blocker taken about 15 to 20 minutes before each meal is enough to block most of the starch in a meal from being converted to sugar. This will allow a person to include some starch back into their diet yet lose the calories.

In many high protein diets almost all fruits and most vegetables have to be excluded as they are high in starch. This then takes out of the diet most vitamins and minerals. By using the starch blocker with meals, fruits and vegetables that are high in starch can be included in the diet so that the vitamins and nutrients from them can be absorbed yet the starch calories can be eliminated.

A second point to this plan is that starch blockers make exercise much more effective. The body prefers to burn carbohydrates as fuel for physical activity. Since it is easy for muscle tissue to metabolize, it is utilized rapidly. Unfortunately most of us do not exercise enough to burn off the calories from carbohydrates in our diet. We barely exercise enough to burn off this morning's bagel or last night's lasagna. By blocking out the starch calories we force the body to burn body fat for fuel during physical activity. Thus body fat that the body has been storing for years or even decades is burned through exercise, instead of burning the "easy" starch calories.

This action of using starch blockers to help the body burn off fat is an extremely useful way of greatly increasing the beneficial effect of any exercise program. We find in our clinical studies that our patients lose not only weight but inches as well. Any type of exercise program thus becomes much more effective with starch blockers. This is an important and extremely useful way of allowing physical activity to burn off excess weight and an important use of starch blockers in controlling weight and promoting good health.

"Diabesity"

An extremely effective use of starch blockers may be its use in what we are beginning to call "diabesity." This is seen as the early onset of obesity leading to diabetes. This continuum begins in childhood or adolescent years as abdominal obesity, progresses to metabolic dysglycemia and Syndrome X, with

www.mentorsmagazine.com

a final result as Type II diabetes. Since starch blockers show a positive effect on weight loss as well as controlling glucose levels and reducing insulin blood levels, this may prove to be an effective method to **prevent** this progressive disease pattern.

Starch blockers have been shown in over forty studies to be safe and effective in promoting healthy weight loss. The added benefits of prevention of "diabesity" and its positive effects on the gastrointestinal system with added fiber make this a uniquely powerful tool in the prevention of chronic diseases and the promotion of good health. Finally there seems to be an effective and safe, natural tool to help fight this growing epidemic of obesity in our country.

Steven Rosenblatt, M.D., Ph.D, LAc, graduated from U.C.L.A. and the prestigious Hong Kong Acupuncture College. Dr. Rosenblatt is the President of Sierra Medicinals, Inc., a company which develops and manufactures nutritional supplements and herbal medications, based on science, for treatment and prevention of chronic illness. His major interest is the utilization and integration of Complementary Medicine in the Western medical clinic to promote health and wellness in the community. Dr. Rosenblatt is the co-author of a book published in April, 2003 by HarperCollins, *The Starch Blocker Diet*. This book is a new approach to diet and health which has generated considerable interest in natural alternative and complementary medicines.

2029 Century Park East, Suite 1112, LA, CA 90067
310-226-2555
www.sierramed.com
email: info@sierramed.com

Positive Addictions Will Postpone Your Funeral

By Kevin E. Brown

I thought I was going to die. The broken and twisted frame of my motorcycle crushed the back of my neck with a thousand pounds of pressure like a reaper's scythe. I lay pinned to the ground, deprived of air, my face forced into the dirt at the bottom of an embankment 40 feet from the road. Panic set in. I knew my only hope for survival was to get back to the road above for help, but my arms and legs were immobilized. With each breath out, less came in. I remember praying, "Please God, I'm not expected home for hours. Who is going to find me? Oh God, please, just let me see the sunrise tomorrow." Taking what I thought was my last breath, I closed my eyes, pictured my wife and said goodbye.

Earlier that morning, the Monet sunrise enticed me to set aside my work. I was in the mood for a ride on my bike. There were so many plans for the future that needed thinking through and nothing quieted my mind more than inhaling the cool summer breeze and feeling the rushing wind on my face. I swung my leg over my gold 1987 Suzuki Cavalcade and knocked the kickstand loose; I loved listening to the familiar roar of the 1500cc engine. It still enthralled me as much as the very first day I rode a motorcycle at the age of four.

As I was driving down the lonely country road in northern Missouri enjoying the spectacular sunrise, I approached an unfamiliar hill with a hazardous left curve at the top. My mind remained occupied with plans for the future, totally oblivious to the danger ahead. My body and bike shot straight ahead, where it should have negotiated the curve to the left. I tumbled over and over down a steep embankment. Wham! The motorcycle landed on my neck as I came to a stop, chest down in the dirt, head turned to the side.

Lying there, resigned to die alone, I heard the most powerful four words of my life: "What can I do?" I didn't know who said them but I did see leather boots, blue jeans and weathered hands from my insect-like perspective. Suddenly, a 74-year-old superman lifted the motorcycle off my body. Immediately my lungs filled with badly needed air and I hungrily gulped it in. My mind cleared. I watched the boots of my rescuer as they paced back and forth, then disappeared as he went to call an ambulance. On his return, he kneeled beside me to ask again, "What can I do?" I really didn't know. It is interesting, in hindsight, that I wasn't in any real pain - just slight discomfort.

www.mentorsmagazine.com

We both agreed that I shouldn't move. As we waited for the ambulance to arrive, he asked me my name. He told me his was J.P. Childers. I asked him how he knew to look over the embankment to find me. He answered, "I was driving along and saw your helmet laying by itself up on the side of the road. So I stopped, frantically searching around, and found you stuck under your bike. As I rushed toward you, I heard you gurgling. I lifted your bike."

"You lifted a thousand pound motorcycle off me?" This is quite amazing because being a very athletic 28-year-old myself, I always had difficulty lifting the motorcycle.

"Yeah, and it wasn't all that heavy either," said Childers. He kept viewing his watch and complaining about the length of time the ambulance was taking to reach me.

SIDE NOTE: We later found out the ambulance had taken a wrong turn and was having trouble finding us. Today, my visits with Mr. Childers begin with him complaining about the driver's delay by not following his specific directions to our accident site. Mr. Childers (my very good friend) will not LET IT GO. It would be very easy for me to have the same feelings, but I have learned this type of thinking causes more harm than good. My question to you is, "What in your world are you stressing over today, this very moment?" If you do come up with something, LET IT GO. Stress is an integral part of all our lives, prematurely aging some, killing others...if you want to postpone your funeral – let it go.

We continued with small talk to relieve the tension. "I guess you weren't wearing your helmet," said Childers, half-asking, half-assuming.

"I always wear my helmet," I said in defense of my usual safety precautions.

"So, how did it come off your head and get up there on the road?" he asked.

We both paused in disbelief. Childers suddenly noticed that the chinstrap was still fastened. It was as if the helmet had been placed on the road as a beacon to bring him to my rescue. To this day, that helmet remains untouched in my study - an important reminder of a higher power beyond man's comprehension.

The Meaning of "Quadriplegic"

I listened to the doctor as he talked past me and told my wife Brenda that I was a quadriplegic. Before the day of the accident, neither Brenda nor I knew the meaning of that word. The doctor explained to her, "That means you will have to feed, bathe and take care of his every need for the rest of his life." In other words, I was paralyzed from the neck down.

I roared back in defiance, "No! I didn't marry a maid or a nurse and I'm not deaf! Please talk to me like I'm in the room!"

"You are still you. Don't worry. We can handle this," Brenda said to me softly.

I agonized over what this would now mean. As I watched Brenda continue to talk softly with the doctor, I remembered back to how we had met. We fell in love in the seventh grade, "going steady" as only kids in junior high school can. We even shared a first kiss to solidify our relationship. As a token of her affection, Brenda had my name printed on a silver identification bracelet. But just when she was about to present it to me, I started going steady with another girl. Brenda and I rarely spoke after that. Some seven years later, a chance meeting at a party brought us back together. Among a gaggle of giggling girls, I noticed her familiar smile. Brenda's eyes seemed to now show signs of forgiveness. I remembered our first kiss. She was even more beautiful than I had remembered. Playing it cool, I headed downstairs to play pool with the guys. Casually, I tested the reactions of my friends with, "Did you guys see Brenda upstairs?"

I was immediately met with well-meaning warnings, trying to protect me from heartbreak. "Don't even think about it. That's Brenda," said Matt. Everyone knew what he meant. Brenda, the Homecoming Queen. Brenda, the girl who's dating the captain of the football team. *THAT IS* BRENDA.

"You are so outclassed, she won't even talk to you. Just forget it."

I was not then, nor am I now, one to allow the words of others to limit my actions.

I not only earned the bracelet back, but a few years passed and we married. Now our love was about to face the test of a lifetime. The doctor turned and asked me, "Do you have a family?"

"Well yes," I said, thinking that was a foolish question. I reminded him that my mother worked at the hospital.

"No," said the doctor, "I mean a family of your own."

The words stuck in my throat. "No, we actually haven't been married very long. We are not at that part of our life yet. We have talked about it a little bit, though."

"Well then, we'll talk to both of you about adoption later. Don't expect to have children of your own." The doctor's words began to thunder in my head as he rambled on with a jumble of statistics from other men with C-5 spinal cord injuries.

Not a day passed that I didn't cry. Everything looked horribly hopeless. I constantly read books that were lighthearted and motivational, watched movies or shows that were funny and built my spirit in every way I could.

Begin Your Personal Health Initiative

The only responsive muscles of my body were in my shoulders, so my physique began to take on a new look. When my stomach began to pouch out, Brenda teased, "You look like a little Buddha." I responded without as much wisdom as Buddha of course, but I knew, even then, that anyone who takes oneself too seriously runs the risk of looking ridiculous. I decided that if I could look in the mirror each morning committed to a healthy life, then I knew I was going to make it. It is a fact that some people are dealt a harder hand than others. It does not seem fair. Yet, who promised life would be fair? The greater question is not: "Why did this happen to me?" But, ultimately, "What will be my response and how will I deal with it?"

My accident became a crash course, *pun definitely intended*, for coming to grips with my own mortality. Once you sense the end of life, you become better equipped to see its miracles. Your health is one of those incredible miracles and you have full control. I later found out that my upbeat attitude had stunned the medical team. What they failed to realize is that you always have a choice. You can focus on your problems or count your blessings. Guess what I do? Which do you choose?

About six months after the accident, I departed Craig Rehab in Colorado, leaving behind 43 fellow patients with spinal cord injuries. The medical team advised that whatever movement I regained during the first six months would be the most I could hope for, and I should expect a life of dependency, a diminished life and a shorter life span.

I seriously doubt when we rely totally on someone else we are at our best. Therefore, I fought for my independence everyday for four years. Where is it written that the importance of life must shrink because of a less than desirable outcome? I simply chose to do more, to give more and ultimately become more. Placing an actual expiration date on my life acted as a catalyst to set daily routines and long-term goals to better my health because a sedentary lifestyle increases the risk of coronary disease.

Determination set the stage for me to make a step forward each day. I had already regained partial use of my triceps, biceps and chest muscles at that time. Today, although I still use a wheelchair, I bench press 149 pounds, snow ski, play full contact wheelchair rugby, biathlon, triathlon, marathon, scuba dive and am totally self-sufficient.

I also cook and clean to boot.

You Truly Do Not Need a Wake Up Call to Finally GET IT.

There was one other prediction I was out to defy. Brenda and I decided to have a child of our own. After only two weeks we managed to conceive. Our miracle child Lauren was born nine months later. The pregnancy and Lauren acted as a catalyst. I realized that this new member of our family changed my priorities. I had an epiphany: "Life is not about walking, it's about doing."

As an ethereal bundle of energy, Lauren is my proudest accomplishment. I never cease to be astounded that I fathered such an incredible child. She knew how to tie her own shoes before age four, was a budding gymnast before age three and brushed her own teeth before age two! Age is an inappropriate excuse. You can always develop Positive Addictions.

As I work on this project, Lauren jumps on my lap to give me one of what she calls "mini-mug (minimum) 4 hugs a day." She continues to chatter with Brenda as she tries to decide on her day. Every morning I revel in the ordinary. I make my daughter breakfast, take her to school, dance, gymnastics and spot her while she does flips on the living room floor.

These are the moments I was told I'd never see. Joy and happiness warm me because I have been blessed to watch the sunrise fill the sky and bask in the light of true prosperity. Life is good if you know what to look for.

Will you do what it takes to postpone your funeral?

The Things That I Have Learned

Initiate Positive Addictions

- Implement this one if you do nothing else. Drink a lake full of *Water* every day for two reasons:

  1. Drinking water is the single most important thing you can do for your organs, your body and your health.

  2. Adequate hydration will keep your cravings at a minimum. Your stomach is full!

- Do you brush your teeth everyday? Why? Exactly. Dental Health. Teeth make up a small portion of your body. Yet, we devote a high percentage of time to their care. So why aren't you exercising everyday? What about your muscles, your heart, or your big bum? Your heart beats over 100,000 times per day, more than 36 million times per year. Show yourself some love. Take a 30-minute stroll. Begin today.

- A great habit for you to begin is eating only fruit during the morning.

- Always snack between meals. Have a cup of grapes (try them frozen -yum!), or four ounces of baked chicken. Constantly eating small portions will keep your metabolism high.

- Reduce your portions. I know, I know... this is easier said than done. Leave at least three bites of all the different foods on your plate. When eating out, ask for a to-go box with your order.

Start today. See your health as the miracle it is. Which one of the above will you implement now? Then, add one new Positive Addiction every two weeks. Soon, you will have a new life chock full of healthy habits.

Quick Tips to De-Stress

1. Turn up the Tunes. Music reduces stress. One medical certainty is that blood pressure surges during the morning hours. However, listening to music can help control it, reducing your chances of a morning coronary. To listen 24/7 go to www.kbia.org and click on classical 24.

2. Meditate 20 minutes everyday. Researchers at Thomas Jefferson University found that 20 minutes of downtime can reduce anxiety levels by more than 25 percent. Use the first 20 minutes after lunch to meditate. Dim your lights, turn off your telephone and quietly sit. If you have had one of those days and you cannot clear your mind, repeat affirmations to yourself. In addition to reducing stress, this will positively affect your self-esteem.

3. Stress less by externalizing your frustrations on an inanimate object. Use a squeeze ball or a punching bag. One Harvard University study found those who express their anger have half the risk of heart disease compared with those who internalize it.

For more, see 101 De-Stress Tips at www.iamkevinbrown.com

Kevin E. Brown: Father, Wheelchair Athlete, Professional Speaker & Author. Kevin, CEO of Shae Communications, serves as a mentor, coach and consultant to enhance your professional and personal life. Get *GREAT FREE STUFF* and daily inspiration. Meeting planners, hire this award-winning speaker today! *www.IamKevinBrown.com* or toll free *866-KevinBrown.*

Independent Thinking:

A Requisite for Good Health

By Julian Whitaker, M.D.

Over the last 25 years we have treated close to 35,000 patients at the Whitaker Wellness Institute in Newport Beach, California. If I could summarize the approach we take with patients, it is two words: orthomolecular medicine. *Orthomolecular* is a term coined by Nobel laureate Linus Pauling, Ph.D. It is defined as "the preservation of good health and the treatment of disease by varying the concentrations in the human body of substances that are normally present in the body and are required for health."

Taking vitamins, minerals, coenzyme Q10 and other nutritional supplements to prevent and treat any disease condition is an example of an orthomolecular therapy. Cutting down on saturated fat and eating more fruits, vegetables and whole grains to maintain and improve health is another example. In both cases, you are modifying the concentrations of the active agents present in supplements and food that have profound effects on health.

Conventional Versus Orthomolecular Therapies

A chief characteristic of orthomolecular therapies is their extremely low level of toxicity. Vitamins, minerals and other nutritional supplements are exceptionally safe, even at large doses. They engender health and treat disease by facilitating the body's ability to correct abnormalities and achieve homeostasis, the balance needed for optimal health.

Drugs (the favorite therapy of conventional physicians) are, on the other hand, quite toxic, even at the usual therapeutic doses. Hundreds of thousands of North Americans die every year from the "appropriate" use of prescription drugs, and millions more are harmed. This is because drugs are xenobiotics, compounds that have never been found in nature. They achieve their desired effects by blocking normal metabolic activities and processes utilized by the body to maintain homeostasis.

So why are drugs conventional medicine's answer to almost everything? It's because natural compounds, even if they work wonders, cannot be patented. Therefore, the financial forces driving modern medicine depend on the almost exclusive use of patented, xenobiotic drugs. It takes independent thought to recognize this because everyday use of prescription drugs has

www.mentorsmagazine.com

become so commonplace that they have become just another part of our culture. Canadians spent $14 billion last year filling more than 335 million prescriptions, and Americans spent an astounding $219 billion on 3.34 billion prescriptions. (Nutritional supplement sales, in contrast, are about 2 percent of drug sales.)

You need to understand that medical school education is virtually underwritten by the pharmaceutical industry. Furthermore, most physicians receive their continuing education from industry-sponsored conferences, journals and promotions. When I was in medical school, I passionately believed that the system of medical education and patient care was pure. If any therapy – be it acupuncture, chiropractic, vitamin and mineral supplementation or medicinal herbs – were of possible value to patients, it would be tested and, if found to be beneficial, incorporated into the system.

I now realize that our current system is far from pure. In spite of their proven value, therapies outside the realm of drugs and surgery are rarely taught in medical schools, nor are they used in hospitals or recommended by physicians. As a result, orthomolecular therapies are, at best, ignored, or, at worst, disparaged and scorned. This is a shame.

Orthomolecular Therapies Work

Orthomolecular therapies are safe, inexpensive therapies that really do work. In fact, for many of our patients, they are nothing short of miraculous. I could fill several books with testimonials from patients who have used orthomolecular therapies to succeed in their fight against disease. Let me tell you about a few of them.

Inez first came to our clinic 16 years ago at the age of 65 after being told that she needed an emergency heart catheterization and likely heart surgery. She was so doped up on medications that she could hardly walk and had to be assisted into the waiting room. We started her on our program of diet, vitamins and minerals, and her response was dramatic. At the end of her two-week stay, she was off all drugs and felt so well that she and her daughter took a five-mile walk on the beach. Inez has continued on this program for more than 16 years. Today, at age 81, she is more active than most half her age. She is also completely off drugs, and, aside from some arthritis, she is in excellent health.

Charmaine was in her late 40s when I first treated her, and she was one of the sickest patients I've ever had. She suffered from congestive heart failure, a condition marked by a weakened, poorly functioning heart and collection of fluid in the lungs and throughout the body. She was taking many medications, was confined to a wheelchair, and she had been told that she had just six months to live. We started her on high doses of coenzyme Q10 and other supplements, and within eight weeks, her heart function dramatically improved. She was able to get out of her wheelchair and had lost 64 pounds of water. The last time I treated Charmaine – some 10 years after she was given six months to live – she was doing great.

Jerome, a schoolteacher with a long history of diabetes, checked out of a hospital against medical advice on the morning he was scheduled to have his left leg amputated because of a severely infected diabetic ulcer. We treated his diabetes with nutritional supplements and diet changes, attended to his ulcer with sugar dressings (an old, forgotten, yet highly effective treatment for wounds) and administered a course of EDTA chelation, a nontoxic intravenous therapy that improves circulation. Today, Jerome is walking on his own two feet.

Georgia, who was suffering from Parkinson's disease, was having such a hard time getting around that she wasn't even sure she could make the trip to our clinic from her home in Oklahoma. Her legs were weak, her left foot was numb and her hands trembled. But she made it, and we immediately started her on intravenous glutathione treatments. Glutathione is the body's premier antioxidant, and IV supplementation can dramatically slow the progress of Parkinson's. Just 48 hours after her first treatment, Georgia's leg weakness resolved, her gait was steadier, sensation returned to her foot and her tremor improved. After leaving our clinic, Georgia continued glutathione therapy with her neurologist at home, and she reports that she's getting better and better.

Patients Must Think for Themselves

I often think about the thousands of patients who have had remarkable results at our clinic during the past 25 years, and I always come back to one thought. Without a doubt, there is extensive scientific validation for the therapies we use, but there is another important factor at work in the healing process: the patient.

Patients who come to the Whitaker Wellness Institute are different. They come here not only because they have heard about our services and results but also because that information sparked something in them that is not present in the overwhelming majority. Almost all of them openly state that they come to us without the consent of their physicians – or against their strongly worded advice to stay away. Often, even their families are dead set against their "reckless behavior," defying conventional thought by coming to a clinic that specializes in the use of natural therapies. What is it that drives these people?

In a single word, it's independence. Patients who come to Whitaker Wellness think for themselves. Some might say they are risk takers, but this is ridiculous. The risks of the surgeries and drugs used in disease care is so much greater than our noninvasive, nontoxic approaches that, in my opinion, the true risk takers are those who follow conventional medical advice.

www.mentorsmagazine.com

Is independent thought necessary for health improvement? You bet it is!

Our current healthcare system is not healthcare at all. It is disease care. Healthcare – showing people how to improve their health, even if they have a disease – doesn't use the tools of disease care that can be organized into multi-billion-dollar enterprises, such as the treatment industries for cancer and heart disease. True healthcare is viciously persecuted by the disease-care industry. In order for any individual to extricate himself from the disease-care institutions that dominate modern medicine and seek out avenues for true healthcare, independent thought is required.

A Framework of Independent Thought

Everyone likes to think they are independent, but independence is only expressed when one truly turns off the congested highway of conventional behavior and takes the road less traveled. I cannot advise you to be an independent thinker – to whatever extent you already are or are not an independent thinker. However, I can give you what I believe may be the framework for independent thought in the field of healthcare. Before you consent to any procedure or therapy, ask these questions.

1. Is the procedure or therapy designed to improve health or stamp out disease?

Does it promote the body's own healing processes and engender long-term health? Let's take the treatment of cardiovascular disease as an example. In conventional medicine, drugs are the first-line therapy, and angioplasty and bypass surgery are popular fallbacks. While these treatments may achieve specific, narrow goals, such as lowering of blood pressure or cholesterol, or reduction of chest pain, do they really improve the course of the disease and enhance overall health? What about the side effects of these treatments, the surgical deaths and debilitation, the adverse events associated with the drugs?

Orthomolecular therapies by their very nature address the underlying disease processes, rather than the symptoms. Folic acid and other B-complex vitamins lower levels of homocysteine, an instigator of atherosclerosis. Fish oil helps prevent arrhythmias of the heart. Coenzyme Q10 supports the heart muscle. Flaxseed helps lower cholesterol, and antioxidants protect against oxidation of LDL cholesterol. Furthermore, these natural agents are nontoxic, and they promote the health of not only the cardiovascular system but also the entire body.

2. Is the healthcare approach reasonable?

Is there a plausible mechanism of action? Here it gets a little tricky because conventional medicine often dismisses orthomolecular therapies as being "unreasonable" and without scientific backing. This is patently false – and those who think independently and are willing to look beyond their doctors' dictates can easily find evidence that the more natural approach works.

If you are open to a drug such as metformin, which lowers blood sugar in patients with diabetes by increasing the cells' sensitivity to insulin, there is no reason not to be open to scientifically proven natural insulin-sensitizing therapies. These include exercise, improved diet and nutritional supplements such as vanadyl sulfate and *Gymnema sylvestre*.

3. Is the approach or therapy natural?

I consider this to be very important. I personally believe that there are far more powerful and beneficial healthcare remedies in the natural world than will ever at any time come out of the pharmaceutical or disease-care world. And from a safety perspective, natural therapies beat drugs and surgery hands down.

Of course, conventional thought would like you to believe that the world is full of hucksters and snake-oil salesmen trying to push potions, nostrums and natural therapies down your throat for a profit. This is no doubt true in some instances. As with anything, you should do your homework when selecting natural therapies. However, these therapies are rapidly coming online in our culture, despite the fact they are at a business disadvantage in that, unlike drugs, none of them can be patented. Even if doctors aren't prescribing them, patients are embracing safe, effective, natural therapies like never before.

Do You Really Want To Be Healthy?

Finally, ask yourself this question: Do you really want to be healthy? Write down what you would do if you were healthier than you are now. How would your life change? What dreams or goals could you achieve?

This simple step is perhaps the most powerful advice I can give. It will provide potent motivation for you to explore avenues that you might not normally take as you walk through the fog of conventional thought.

Dr. Julian Whitaker is a pioneer in the fields of alternative and complementary medicine, and has been in practice for more than 30 years. He is the author of many books as well as the editor of *Health & Healing*, a monthly newsletter that provides health advice to hundreds of thousands of subscribers.
www.drwhitaker.com or 800-488-1500

Purslane –
The Plant That Heals

By Elsie Belcheff

Purslane (Portulaca) Oleracea is a low growing succulent annual plant with branches 4 - 18" long. It has small yellow flowers, which produce many sand-sized black seeds. It has been used for centuries in countries throughout the world as both a basic food and for medicinal purposes to great effect.

Among 13,000 known plants, fewer than twenty are currently providing most of our food needs, yet many of the under utilized plants - such as Purslane- offer better nourishment than the major crops. Coquillat M.: 1951:165 studies rated Purslane as the eighth most common plant in the world. Holm LG, Pluckette et al, University of Hawaii 1977, stated that Purslane is one of three most frequently reported weeds across the world.

What Purslane Has to Offer

On Dec. 1, 2000, an analysis study of Purslane Powder at Saskatoon, P.O.S. Plant at University of Saskatchewan, Canada, Lab found the plant high in:

1) **Fatty Acids.** Omega 3 and Omega 6 are essential for growth, cell development and anti-inflammation. They are now linked to a decrease in risk factors for heart disease and a lessening of symptoms of other afflictions including psoriasis, rheumatoid arthritis, diabetes, and more.

2) **Found tocopherol (beta, gamma, and delta) Vitamin E compounds.** Only alpha – tocopherol is produced commercially both in natural and synthetic forms. The other three tocopherols (beta, gamma and delta) are available only in their natural forms. Also the tocotrionols (alpha, beta, gamma and delta) are available commercially only in their natural forms. There are no synthetic tocotrionols available.

Numerous studies have been done on natural Vitamin E vs. synthetic Vitamin E. The differences are big and very real. There is a difference between natural and synthetic in the molecule. There is a difference in its potency. There is a difference in how it behaves in the body. And there is a major difference in how it goes from the mother to the baby in the womb.

"Natural doesn't mean much when it comes to vitamins, with Vitamin E probably the only exception." – New York Times – February 3, 1993

"The results indicated that natural Vitamin E has roughly twice the availability of synthetic Vitamin E." – Dr. Graham W. Burton, National Research Council of Canada

Fortunately, synthetic alpha-tocopherol is not harmful. But its value to our body is only half that of the natural. Our bodies are water-based, therefore water-based Vitamin E absorbs more readily into our bodies.

3) **Alpha-tocopherol.** In Dr. A. Simopoulous studies, alpha-tocopherol found in Purslane in dry weight is up to ten times higher than has been recorded in other plants researched.

4) **Beta-Carotene (Vitamin A), Vitamin C, niacin and riboflavin.**

5) **Minerals.** Purslane contains phosphorus, zinc, iron, silicon, manganese, copper, calcium and magnesium.

6) **Salts.** Studies by Kabulov and Tashbekov have found Purslane rich in different salts, especially in proteins and carbohydrates.

7) **Anti-oxidants.** The antioxidant activity found in dried Purslane was two-fold more effective than commercial cranberry and grape seed products. Purslane was found to be an excellent source of anti-oxidants, such as Vitamin C, E and Beta Carotene, glutathione, potassium and pectin (known to lower cholesterol).

Purslane and Anti-Oxidants

What are anti-oxidants? Anti-oxidants are reactions that help to neutralize the damage of oxidation in the body. Oxidation in our bodies is similar to what happens to metal when it rusts, or to an apple when it turns brown. This oxidization is caused by many things, but the major causes are in air and water pollution, industrial chemicals, cigarette smoke, drugs, poor diets and rancid oils. Antioxidants also help the body fight disease and the effects of aging, yet few Americans and Canadians are getting enough of them.

Purslane (Oleracea) was found high in glutathione – an antioxidant and detoxifying agent that has been demonstrated in various chemical studies. Glutathione is now known to be widely distributed in plant cells. It is a ubiquitous compound that is synthesized readily in the liver, kidneys and other tissues, including the gastrointestinal tract. Recent studies show that glutathione obtained from the diet is directly absorbed by the gastrointestinal tract, and thus dietary glutathione can readily increase the antioxidant status in humans.

Glutathione may protect cells from carcinogenic processes through a number of mechanisms:

1) by functioning as an antioxidant
2) by binding with mutagenic chemical compounds
3) by directly or indirectly acting to maintain functional levels of other

antioxidants such as Vitamin C and E and B-Carotene
4) through its involvement in DNA synthesis and repair
5) by enhancing the immune response (adapted from Jones et al 1992)

Anti-oxidants such as those found in Purslane are vital in the battle against free radicals. Free radicals damage the cell's membrane, interfering with its ability to send and receive messages from other cells and to absorb necessary nutrients while eliminating waste products. Free radicals also damage a cell's nucleic acid, DNA, and mitochondria. Mitochondria are the cell's power plan, furnishing the energy needed by cells and tissues to properly function. Deficits of energy cause greater fatigue and pain, and cause organs to function at a reduced capacity.

Free radical damage is most noticeable in oxygen-rich organs (eyes, brain, liver, heart, kidneys and blood) and has been implicated in the following diseases: kidney disease, diabetes, pancreatic, liver damage, chrones & colitis disease, inflammation of the gastrointestinal tract, lung disease, eye diseases, Parkinson's, Alzheimer's, multiple sclerosis, diseases affecting red blood cells (sickle cell anemia, pernicious anemia), iron overload, autoimmune diseases (rheumatoid arthritis, lupus) and most infections (tuberculosis, malaria, AIDS).

What Purslane Can Do

Purslane has been studied extensively by Artemis P. Simopoulos of the U.S. Centre of Genetics, Nutrition and Health in Washington, D.C. She is recognized as one of the world's leading nutritional authorities regarding Purslane. Her research commented: "Purslane has been shown many times to contain the richest source of linoliec acid (LNA) Omega 3 of any green leafy vegetable yet examined. Dried Purslane has about 5 times more Vitamin E than does spinach."

Simopoulous has demonstrated that Omega-3 fatty acids are essential for growth and development and are responsible for traditional/historical health benefits for various acute chronic conditions such as:

1) muscle relaxant effect;
2) anti-thrombotic (prevents blood platelet clotting);
3) hypolipedemic (promotes normal lipid metabolism);
4) hypotensive (promotes normal blood pressure);
5) skin soothing emollient;
6) anti-bacterial;
7) anti-fungal;
8) wound, boils and burn healing;
9) anti-inflammatory;
10) arthritis;
11) headaches;

12) shortness of breath;

13) cardiac tonic (i.e., improves heart contractions);

14) as a cooling medicine for fevers (febrifuge);

15) anthelminic (anti-parasitic);

16) cathartic (promotes bowel evacuation);

17) diuretic (to promote the formation and excretion of urine, typically used to reduce the volume of extracellular fluid in the treatment of many disorders including hypertension, congestive heart failure and edema/ swelling).

Furthermore, scientists Feng et al have shown in their research that Purslane (Portulaca) also contains high amounts of nor adrenaline, which may even be higher in concentration than what is extractable from the suprarenal glands from mammals. Scientist Hegnauer in 1969 reported that aqueous extracts of Purslane contain dopa, dopamine, catecholamines and noradrenaline.

The adrenal acts as the body's energy reserve tank. These two triangular glands sitting above the kidneys are responsible for overall health and vitality, since they control all hormone functioning. Each of these glands is divided into two parts, an inner section called the medulla and an outer layer called the cortex.

The adrenal medulla produces a set of hormones called catecholamines – the stress hormone and dopamine – all of which play an important role in the way we respond to danger, intense emotion, low blood sugar, extreme temperature, oxygen shortage, low blood pressure and stress. In addition, the adrenals support immunity, determine red and white blood cell counts, and in blood clotting, and control voluntary muscles, bodily strength, the heart muscles, blood pressure, uterine tone, and involuntary muscle contractions (peristalsis).

Essential Amino Acids

Miller et al, 1984 research shows that Purslane oleracea seed and leaves have a good balance and a good concentration of essential amino acids, more than in any other plant researched. What is the importance of essential amino acids? Amino acids are the building blocks of protein. The essential amino acids are:

- Isoleucine – aids in energy production and hemoglobin formation
- Loucine – helps heal injured or weakened muscle, fractured or weakened bones, and skin conditions
- Valine – used by the body to produce energy
- Methionine – a potent antioxidant
- Threonine – stimulates immune system and thymus gland activity
- Phenylalanine – precursor of the neurotransmitters dopamine and norepinephrine

- Tryptophan – precursor of the neurotransmitters serotonin and melatonin

Purslane vs. Cancer

A patent has been issued by the U.S. Patent office to Yoom et al Calgary, Calgary #589,060; Date of Patent February 9, 1999, regarding Purslane (Oleracea) and Tumor Cell Growth. In the abstract it is disclosed Purslane has a specific and distinct effect on the inhibition and/or suppression of gastric tumor cell growth in vitro and vivo. An aqueous extract of Purslane showed a tumericidal activity against KATO 11 (human gastric carcinoma cell) and calo 320 HSR cells (human colon adenoma cell line) in a dose – dependent and time, but not against the non – tumorous cell liner. This means that Purslane is not attacking healthy cells (no side effects), but only attacks the tumor cells.

Medicinal Uses of Purslane in Other Countries

Columbia – Emollient on tumors, calluses

Philippines – Heal burns, skin disease

China – Emollient, leaves used as poultice (hot herb pack) for tumors, bad wounds and ulcers, whereas the seeds are considered a diuretic

Gold Coast – Leaves ground, mixed with oil, used on boils to bring them to a head

West Tropical Africa – Leaves used as a poultice on boils and burns, and as heart tonic and diuretic

Nigeria – Leaves applied to swellings

Siberia – Eaten as a regular food, used as a gastric sedative herb, for prickly heat, applied to forehead and temple to relieve heat and pain, applied to eyes to remove inflammation

West Indies, Cochin, China – The Tamil practitioners use seeds for stomach problems, to provoke menses; also as an emollient and diuretic. The bruised fresh leaves are used externally for erysipelas

Guadelupe, Corre, Lejanne – The whole plant is used as a tonic and febrifuge (for fevers)

Jamaica – The plant is given as a 'cooling medicine' for fevers

North America – The whole plant is used as a cooling diuretic, whereas the seeds are considered to be anthelminthic (anti-parasitic)

Punjab – Seeds are used as a vermifuge

Punjab and Cashmere – Seeds are used by the hakims in inflammation of the stomach and intestinal ulcerations

Conclusion

Studies clearly show that Purslane is an excellent source of fatty acids Omega 3 & 6 (LNA), Vitamin E (tocopherol beta, gamma, and delta and alpha-tocopherol), Vitamin C, beta-carotene (Vit A), riboflavin, potassium, amino acids, gluthione, pectin, minerals (phosphorus, zinc, silicon, manganese, copper, calcium, magnesium and Co-enzyme Q-10, which is found in every cell of the body known to supply our bodies with energy), all of which may contribute to the medicinal uses of Purslane as a cardiac tonic, diuretic, against infections of the skin and disorders of the gastrointestinal tract and more. Because of the well balanced, rich nutrients in this plant, Purslane is considered to be a **Power Food of the Future.**

Elsie Belcheff, Certified Herbologist from Margo, Saskatchewan, Canada. Belcheff is the founder of Natural Plantation, manufacturer of the top selling products made from pure Purslane Portulaca (Oleracea) Powder. Purslane Portulaca is known for its medicinal uses. For more information, go to the website at www.naturalplantation.com OR call toll free at 1-866-806-4372 or e-mail at info@naturalplantation.com.

Staying
Mentally Sharp

By Michael A. Schmidt, Ph.D.

The last few years have brought some of the most surprising, if not stunning, revelations in our understanding of how the brain works and how to keep it functioning at its peak. While there are many influences on brain health that range from love and intimacy to genes and exercise, one of the most surprising discoveries surrounding mental and emotional well being has become evident only recently: your brain's health is powerfully influenced by your waistline.

This is an extraordinary idea: that the waistline may affect the brain. Yet if we examine recent studies with humans and probe deeply into the secret lives of fat cells as we now understand them, the effect begins to make sense.

MENTOR
#16

Some of the most striking evidence of the potential belly-brain association came in February 2003. Scientists used magnetic resonance imaging to scan a portion of the brain critical to memory called the *hippocampus*. This part of the brain is known to be particularly vulnerable to things like impaired blood sugar balance, free radical stress, sleep deprivation and psychological stress. Scientists wanted to see if problems related to blood sugar regulation affected the actual size of this key memory center.

The scientists discovered that people with impaired glucose tolerance (problems with blood sugar regulation) had smaller memory centers (hippocampi). They also administered tests that showed memory impairment and poor mental performance when compared to people with normal glucose tolerance. It's important to note that impaired glucose tolerance is commonly associated with a larger waistline and increased belly fat.

Then, again in 2003, scientists in Sweden made another startling find. Older women who had a body mass index (BMI) over 29 had a higher risk of developing Alzheimer's disease in the next five years. Women with healthier BMIs (less than 25) did not have an increased risk. To put this in perspective, a woman who is 5-feet, 4-inches and 170 pounds would have a BMI of 29. A 5-foot, 4-inch woman who was 145 pounds would have a BMI of 25. In short, the larger the BMI, the greater the risk of Alzheimer's.

While the link between a bigger waistline, increased belly fat and brain aging requires further research, there is ample reason to believe the effects are real because belly fat is a virtual engine of inflammation.

We used to view fat cells as dull, dormant or inactive storage facilities. We knew the more fat you accumulated the larger your waistline grew. That was obvious. But new research shows that fat cells are far from dormant. In fact, they release some of the same inflammatory chemicals that your body releases when it has an infection or has been in a car accident: chemicals that are usually made by white blood cells. These chemicals with cumbersome names such as C-reactive protein, interleukin-1 beta, interleukin-6 and tumor necrosis factor alpha (TNFα), all contribute to inflammatory damage that affects the health and longevity of the brain. They also contribute to poor glucose tolerance, the very thing that damaged the memory centers in the first study mentioned above.

But what causes the sequence that leads to increased belly fat, increased inflammation and, perhaps, declining brain function? *Part* of the answer may lie in a now-familiar debate: the carbohydrate controversy.

Sorting Out the Carbohydrate Confusion

While it's true that sugars can improve memory and cognition in the short term, when taking tests for example, we must now pay close attention to the potential serious effects of sugars and carbohydrates on the long-term health of the brain.

Glycemic Index (GI) is a measure of the degree to which a carbohydrate is likely to raise your blood sugar (glucose) levels. The scale is 0 to 100 (based on either white bread or glucose), with 0 being low and 100 being high. In a recent study, 244 healthy women were tested to see how their GI (the intake of high or low glycemic foods) affected an inflammation chemical called CRP (C-reactive protein). Women with high glycemic diets had average CRP values of 5.0 while those with low glycemic diets had CRP levels of only 1.6. The highest levels were in women who were overweight. This suggests high glycemic carbohydrates can contribute to inflammation that is unhealthy for the brain. Imagine, carbohydrates fueling inflammation. It gets even more interesting.

When 21 people were given 75 grams of glucose (about the amount of sugar in two soft drinks), the free radical products, called isoprostanes, rose by 34 percent in only 90 minutes. A separate study showed that people with impaired glucose tolerance had a significant increase in blood levels of other inflammation chemicals such as TNF and IL-6 after a simple sugar load. The sugar load also depleted one of the brain's protective antioxidants: glutathione.

The isoprostane issue is interesting because in a separate study published in the *Archives of Neurology*, mild isoprostane elevation was associated with mild cognitive impairment, while significant isoprostane elevation was associated with Alzheimer's disease.

What these studies tell us is that sugars and refined carbohydrates (also high glycemic carbs) can increase the free radical stress and inflammatory stress on the body, which may accelerate some of the functional losses we typically associate with brain aging.

Fructose and Peak Brain Performance

I noted above that people with impaired glucose tolerance (insulin resistance) had smaller memory centers in the brain (smaller hippocampi) than people with normal glucose tolerance. But just how does one develop glucose intolerance (insulin resistance)?

While there are several complex reasons, I'll focus on just one for the moment: the dietary sugar called *fructose*. Fructose has become the most prevalent sweetener in the diet because it's sweeter than sucrose (common table sugar). It is often recommended because, on the glycemic index, it measures a paltry 32.

But we've been fooled for years by fructose and its low glycemic index. It turns out that consuming fructose has a dark side for the brain and the body in general. Scientists have found that feeding fructose actually *creates* insulin resistance. Rats fed fructose for only eight weeks, had serum insulin levels three times higher than normal. This means the body was failing at regulating its blood sugar and made more insulin than normal to try and correct it. This state of affairs, insulin resistance, is the same circumstance under which the human subjects developed smaller memory centers in their brains in the study mentioned earlier.

Fructose also increases free radical stress, hypertension, elevated triglycerides and weight gain – none of which are healthy for the brain. In fact, these effects are so predictable that many scientists now use fructose to induce these conditions in animals so that they can study drugs that might correct them.

Foods That May Influence Brain Inflammation

Increasingly, inflammation and free radical stress appear to be the enemies of peak brain performance and brain longevity. This is one reason that foods with antioxidant potential have garnered so much attention of late.

A group of scientists at the University of California, Berkeley set out to see if there was a relationship between fruit and vegetable consumption and blood levels of CRP and isoprostanes in 292 healthy people. Remember, CRP is an inflammatory chemical and isoprostanes are free radical-related end products damaging to the brain. The scientists learned that people with the highest blood levels of carotenoids (beta-carotene, alpha-carotene, lutein, zeaxanthin and cryptoxanthin) had the lowest levels of isoprostanes. Another study showed these same antioxidants seemed to protect against impaired glucose tolerance.

Essential Fatty Acids

While the list of nutrients that affect brain performance are too numerous to mention here, there is one family of nutrients so vital to brain function that it must garner special attention: essential fatty acids.

A little-known fact is that the brain is almost 60 percent fat (by dry weight). The fatty acids in the brain are highly organized, immensely complex and vital to its function. The brain is highly dependent upon very specific kinds of fatty acids. Vary the type of fatty acids in the diet over time, and you may vary the actual structure of the brain. This impact begins in the womb and holds true for the entirety of one's life.

A recent analysis of many studies examining the effect of fat on brain function shows that consuming high levels of saturated fat and warm weather oils (like safflower and sunflower) appears to have a negative effect on memory and cognition. Consuming cold water fish (salmon, mackerel, herring, sardines) or fatty acid supplements had a beneficial effect on memory and cognition. Omega-3 fatty acids, those found in cold water fish and fish oil, are among the most crucial to the brain and are among the most commonly deficient in the diet.

One reason omega-3 fatty acids may benefit the brain is that they affect inflammation. In one study, those who had higher levels of the omega-3 fatty acid DHA in their blood had lower levels of the inflammatory chemical CRP. Another study showed high levels of DHA in the blood protected against the development of Alzheimer's disease over the ensuing 10 years. So, not only is the fatty acid DHA required to build and maintain brain tissue, it also appears to lower inflammation.

Exercise and Inflammation

Aside from all the benefits of exercise we are familiar with, there is another: exercise seems to *lower* inflammation. In one study of the inflammatory chemical C-reactive protein, 30 percent of those who did not exercise had elevated CRP levels. Of those who exercised vigorously on a regular basis, only 8 percent had elevated CRP levels.

Other studies suggest that, if your inflammatory markers are too high, exercise (or losing weight) seems to lower them. This applies to a series of inflammatory chemicals such as TNF, IL-1, and IL-6. Briefly, regular moderate to vigorous exercise can reduce belly fat, lower inflammation chemicals and other risk factors that influence peak performance of your brain over time.

Sleep and the Brain

Sleep, belly fat and brain performance also appear to share an intimate relationship. If you consider the study mentioned at the outset of this chapter, that those with impaired glucose tolerance were shown by MRI to have smaller memory centers in the brain, the recent findings about sleep and glucose tolerance are a bit sobering. When young men were exposed to sleep-deprived conditions, their ability to take up sugar (the brain's primary fuel) into the brain fell significantly. Also, the young men's response to a normal carbohydrate meal at breakfast was similar to that of elderly men. This reflected impaired glucose tolerance – the same thing found in the study of the smaller hippocampi mentioned above. Sleep deprivation also caused the cortisol (stress) response in these healthy young men to be similar to that of an elderly person. Cortisol has been shown, in other studies, to damage the memory center in the brain.

Another aspect of the sleep equation is growth hormone. We know growth hormone is needed for retaining peak brain performance and brain longevity (I won't go into all the reasons). Roughly 60 to 70 percent of your body's growth hormone is secreted during the early phases of sleep – called slow wave sleep. Scientists have found that even partial sleep deprivation is associated with reduced growth hormone and increased cortisol. Both of these are hallmarks of aging, but can occur in a younger person who doesn't get enough sleep or who doesn't get enough deep sleep early in the evening.

Higher body mass index and larger waistlines have also been found to be associated with loss of slow-wave sleep, the kind needed to bolster your growth hormone and reduce your stress hormone levels. In another strange twist, people with larger waistlines are more prone to sleep apnea. It has been learned in recent years that those with sleep apnea release more inflammatory chemicals and have more free radical stress present in the brain.

What You Can Do

My strategies for improving brain performance have emerged from several avenues of experience, including my work at NASA examining the physiological and biochemical responses to biological stress conditions. For 15 years I have also been conducting biochemical profiles on people with all sorts of issues related to brain and physical performance, and from work with neural imaging.

This work, combined with the research performed by others, leads me to believe that, no matter whether you are an astronaut, an office worker, an elite athlete, a person who has slowly become overweight, or almost anyone else, you have immense control over preserving your brain's performance.

The above discussion only scratches the surface of the evidence that seems to build each day. We have much to learn. Yet if I were to describe a simple strategy from what we know today that would offer potential advantages to preserving and optimizing brain health and performance, it would include the following:

1. Strive to keep your belly fat in check. Attempt to get your waistline below 35 inches, if at all possible for men; less than 30 inches for women.
2. Exercise three to six times per week. Combine aerobic exercise with resistance exercises such as weights – dumbbells are exceptionally helpful.
3. Go to sleep before 9 p.m., if you can; 10 p.m. is okay, but don't routinely push bedtime past 10 p.m.
4. Eat several servings of fruit daily, especially blueberries, strawberries, blackberries and raspberries. The high antioxidant content offers some degree of neuro-protection.
5. Eat several servings of vegetables daily, including spinach, kale, Brussels sprouts, carrots, squash, pumpkin and others. These confer further antioxidant protection to the brain.
6. Use spices in cooking that have known anti-inflammatory activity such as ginger, thyme, oregano, turmeric, rosemary, onion and garlic. These are known to inhibit several of the inflammatory pathways that adversely affect the brain.
7. Ensure you get the appropriate essential fatty acids in your diet. Several studies now show that omega-3 fatty acids such as EPA and DHA have critical roles in the brain. They are commonly deficient in Western diets and are found in cold water fish: salmon, mackerel, herring, sardines, anchovies and blue fin tuna. Fish oil supplements ensure adequate omega-3 fatty acid intake.
8. Watch your refined carbohydrate intake (simple sugars), especially if you are already overweight. Also, watch your total carbohydrate intake from all sources. Carbohydrates in excess have been related to increased production of inflammatory compounds in the body.
9. Avoid consumption of fructose in all packaged or bottled foods (listed on labels as fructose, high fructose corn syrup and corn syrup). Though fructose has a low glycemic index, its other properties cause it to impair glucose tolerance and increase oxidative stress – harmful to the brain in the long term.

These are all things I do personally and things I counsel patients on, whether they are professional athletes, adults with mood or memory disorders or children with developmental problems. While they appear simple and you've likely heard them before, our new understanding of their effect on whole body inflammation and the brain makes our attention to them all the more urgent.

Dr. Michael A. Schmidt did his Ph.D. research in molecular medicine and neuroscience at NASA Ames Research Center. He is the author of *Brain-Building Nutrition* and the forthcoming *Nutritional Pharmacology and Clinical Neuroscience*. He is a Research Fellow at the Living Longer Center and ProScan Imaging in Cincinnati, Ohio.
www.livinglonger.com

The 8 Steps to Optimum
Energy & Vitality

By Brad J. King, M.S., MFS

My two-year-old nephew came for a visit the other day. The little guy didn't stop moving – walking, running, crawling, jumping, or bouncing – for five hours straight. When it was time to leave, his parents were less than thrilled. I had wound him up so much that he would probably need another hour or two to get back to "normal." (I love being an uncle!)

"All the wonders that you seek are within yourself." – Sir Thomas Brown (1605-82)

Watching my nephew got me thinking: When it comes to energy levels, what is "normal," anyway? Unfortunately, the majority of North Americans no longer know what optimum energy or vitality – true health – feels like. Worse, they probably don't know what they're missing. They think they're designed to feel the way they do – tired, listless, lethargic. In other words, they think they feel "normal!"

"In every moment, the quality of your life is on the line. In each, you are either fully alive or relatively dead." – Dan Millman

But lethargy and fatigue aren't "normal." Your body – like my nephew's – was designed to produce loads of optimum energy, at any age. If you're not feeling optimally energetic, chances are you've been gumming up the system and shutting down billions of your cellular engines for a while without knowing it. Fortunately, you can regain your lost energy potential.

"Oz never did give nothin' to the Tin Man that he didn't already have." – America, Tin Man

We blame everything on our genes these days. As we learn more and more about the human body and its interactions with its environment, however, it becomes increasingly clear that our lifestyle and dietary choices are likely far more important to our health than our genetic makeup. In his groundbreaking book Genetic Nutritioneering, Jeffrey Bland, Ph.D., explains that our genetic inheritance is little more than a template upon which we build our unique life experiences. While our genetic codes may be fixed, their expression changes constantly, adapting to diet, lifestyle, and environment. To a very large extent, you choose whether you'll express your genes towards health or disease — towards vibrant energy or lack thereof.

"So often times it happens that we live our lives in chains and we never even know we have the key." – Eagles, *Already Gone*

It's never too late to teach your body how to be vital and energetic again. It's time to demand more than the "normalcy" of mediocrity. Accept nothing but the best from a body that was designed to take you through life at maximum capacity. In the following eight steps, I will guide you through the most important strategies for tapping into your unlimited energy potential and reawakening the energetic two-year-old within.

"The last thing we usually respect is the one thing we can't live without – our body." – Brad J. King

The 8 Steps to Optimum Energy & Vitality

Step 1: Believe You Can

Sir William Drummond said, "He who will not reason is a bigot; he who cannot is a fool; and he who dares not is a slave."

Are you a slave to your limiting self-beliefs?

We often limit ourselves with false beliefs that we accept as undeniable truths – for example, that we're too old, too out of shape, too far gone, too lazy or lethargic to experience optimum health. Many of us steer ourselves toward failure because of these beliefs.

In order to transform your life, you must first and foremost get rid of these false, limiting self-beliefs. Your self-image guides your habits, so if you see yourself as a lethargic, unhealthy person, then you'll be lethargic and unhealthy. When you consciously try to trade negative habits and ideas for positive ones, your self-image will eventually accept these habits and ideas as reality. Act as if you're already the person you want to be.

"Watch your thoughts; they become words. Watch your words; they become actions. Watch your actions; they become habits. Watch your habits; they become character. Watch your character; it becomes your destiny." – Frank Outlaw

Step 2: Drink More Water

You are mostly water. Water makes up 75% of the brain and muscles, 80% of the blood and lungs – even your bones are 25% water. Next to oxygen, water is the most important nutrient for sustaining life. It is essential to cellular energy production, slowing down the aging process, and helping us lose excess body fat. Studies show that for every pound of fluid lost, the body produces energy less efficiently – not good when we're trying to boost energy!

Yet many of us are dehydrated and don't even know it! Oh sure, we drink plenty of liquids all right – juice, coffee, tea and soda pop – but none of these come anywhere near the myriad health benefits associated with water. According to Dr. Batmanghelidj, the author of *Your Body's Many Cries for Water*,

103

and a world authority in the area of water biochemistry, many people overeat because they believe they are hungry, when in fact they may actually be thirsty and not even know it! As we age, the signals that are sent to the brain for both hunger and thirst often become mixed. This is one of the reasons I have my own clients drink a full glass of water approximately 20 minutes before each meal (in order to assure they don't overeat).

Do your body a favor and consume a minimum of eight full (8 oz.) glasses of water each and every day. Try carrying water with you wherever you go. Commit to drinking nothing but water for one full week. If you'd like, add lemon or lime (preferably organic) for taste. After a week you won't want to drink anything else.

"They suffer because they do not know they are thirsty." – Dr. Batmanghelidj, *Bio-Age: 10 Steps to a Younger You*

Step 3: Choose Food Wisely

Every minute of every day, your body rebuilds, replaces and replenishes about 200 million cells. And it gets the raw materials for this function from the food you eat. Every time you put something in your mouth, therefore, you choose your body's building materials. Junk food builds a junk body – period!

I could write (and have written) volumes about food choices. Suffice it to say that your diet should include a wide variety of fruits and vegetables (preferably organic), high-quality protein (game meat and organic grass-fed beef, organic free-run chicken and eggs, organic yogurt and fish), and "good" fats (organic butter, monounsaturated oils like olive and avocado, and omega-3 fats found in flax seeds and cold-water fish oils).

It's also important to realize the power of incorporating protein into every meal and eating smaller quantities of food at regular intervals (five or six times a day) throughout the day. By following this strategy, you will balance your blood-sugar levels (virtually eliminating cravings) and maintain an optimum hormonal profile for abundant energy.

Socrates once said, "Thou shouldst eat to live; not live to eat." Next time you sit down to eat, try giving your food your full attention. (Hint: turn off the TV for a change!) We should all learn to eat as though our lives depended upon it – because they do!

"Tell me what you eat, and I will tell you what you are." – Anthelme Brillat-Savarin, *The Physiology of Taste*, 1825

Step 4: Never Diet

One plausible reason that so many diets fail is that most of them focus on losing weight; not on losing fat. Too often, the lost weight comes from lean tissue or muscle. Since muscle is a key fat-burner (with the power to incinerate many extra calories in a day) and energy booster, dieting erodes a valuable source of energy and vitality. If would-be Fat Warriors focused on losing energy-sucking fat and preserving and building lean body tissues (especially muscle), there would be a lot more diet "success stories" out there – and a lot more energy and vitality to go around!

Dieting is a short-term solution to a lifelong problem. To lose fat and build muscle – and to look and feel great – you need to make wise eating and regular exercise part of your whole life, not just part of a two-week "diet plan." So get off the diet and get on with your life!

"All dieting accomplishes is turning you into a smaller fat person." – Brad J. King

Step 5: Move Your Body

The human body is designed to move! Studies confirm that reduced activity levels strongly correlate to lost energy and strength and increases in body fat.

Don't worry: proper physical exercise doesn't necessarily mean hardcore sports or lifting mind-numbingly heavy weights. It can be performing moderate resistance exercises in a fitness centre or in the privacy of your own home two to four times a week for only 30 to 45 minutes. In a groundbreaking 1990 study presented in the prestigious Journal of the American Medical Association, even 90-year-old women showed greatly improved muscle size and strength after as little as eight weeks of weight training. And if nice little old ladies can do it, what's stopping you?

The message? Exercise is not optional if you want to experience optimum energy and vitality. Instead of parking it, take your body for a spin!

"People don't die of old age; they die of neglect." – Jack LaLanne

Step 6: Sleep More

Your lost energy potential might be a good night's sleep away. Proper sleep is essential to replenish energy reserves, rebuild and repair muscle tissue, re-energize the immune system, and cleanse the brain of excess cellular debris. Sleep loss has a cumulative – and disastrous – effect on the overall outcome of energy production.

All bodily processes revolve around the intricate timing of nature's clock – sunrise and sunset, or the circadian rhythms of nature. Staying up late or missing valuable sleep puts us out of sync with nature's clock, causing hormonal rhythms to run amok and energy levels to decline precipitously.

So start making a good night's sleep (at least eight hours) one of your highest priorities – your life depends on it.

www.mentorsmagazine.com

Step 7: Stress Less

Many top medical researchers agree that stress may be the primary cause of many illnesses today.

During a stress response, the body produces powerful hormones designed to save your life in times of danger by increasing heart rate and muscle strength and heightening senses. But your stress response wasn't designed to stay on for extended periods of time. Constantly activated, it eventually destroys your cellular systems and depletes your body's energy potential – one reason why people tend to age drastically during short periods of major stress.

In the face of stress, perception equals reality. In other words, whether you're running away from an attacker or worrying about your unpaid bills, your body reacts the same way – by pumping out harmful, energy-zapping, illness-promoting stress hormones. In order to rebuild your energy reserves, you must learn to face stressful events with some degree of calm.

"I have been through some terrible things in my life, some of which actually happened." – Mark Twain

Step 8: Don't Wait

Johann Wolfgang von Goethe said, "Whatever you can do, or dream you can, begin it. Boldness has genius, power and magic in it." Don't put off change – life is way too short! Health is no different. If you constantly wait for the perfect moment to begin, you may never start.

"Why wait? Life is not a dress rehearsal. Quit practicing what you're going to do, and just do it. In one bold stroke you can transform today." – Marilyn Grey

Brad J. King, M.S., MFS, is a nutritional researcher, fitness expert, and author of the International best seller *Fat Wars: 45 Days To Transform Your Body*. He has appeared as a leading expert on national radio and television shows, including the Today Show. For more information and to sign up for a free monthly *Fat Wars Chronicle* visit: www.fatwars.com

Appetite for the Ultimate Food

By Dr. Donald M. McLeod
and Dr. Philip A. White

Food is more than mere sustenance. Since the dawn of man, food has had a deeper intrinsic spiritual meaning. Every religious, personal, or nationalistic celebration encompasses food. Just think of birthday, Valentine's, Halloween and "going away" parties, all with specific palatable treats. It is true "we are what we eat and we eat to get to where we are!"

Humans have been struggling with diets for hundreds of thousands of years. The original diets didn't require much thought. Whatever could be safely eaten and smelled or tasted good was incorporated. As humans lived in larger groups and combined their talents and energies, foodstuffs multiplied. We progressively moved away from hunting and gathering towards farming of both plants and animals. Carbohydrates, once very scarce except as a product of wild fruit, berries, grains and vegetables, crept into the main menu. The advent of cheap, liberally available carbohydrates forever changed the way humans satisfy hunger and energy needs. Our evolutionary ability to gain weight in the form of abdominal fat is virtually carbohydrate specific. We were DESIGNED so we could (and still can) gain pounds from carbohydrates to sustain us when food was scarce. We do not need that today, as one season is virtually indistinguishable from the next in what is available for food. Instead, we pack on abdominal fat and subsequently develop diabetes via insulin resistance. Advanced glycosylated end products (AGEs) result from too much sugar attaching to proteins, disturbing our biochemistry.

Carefully selecting our diet is an obvious choice for the best chance of disease-free aging. The adage "moderation in all things" may be the key. Avoiding chemical toxins and poisons in the environment and fulfilling the brain and body's need for nutrients to repair ongoing damage are fundamental. Providing the right fuel to power this human machine with minimal waste accumulating in the cells is paramount.

Caloric restriction has been demonstrated as a prescription for longevity, but does it create optimal human performance? The Vikings of yesteryear and the modern Olympic athletes of today don't think so. Their high protein and high calorie diets achieve maximal non-fat body mass and as a result, performance. But being overweight (54 percent of Americans) or obese (31

percent of Americans) may account for 20 percent of cancers today. This is especially true for women. Recent studies have shown overfed pre-term infants achieving too much weight gain will end up with insulin resistance, resulting in diabetes and cardiovascular disease at a surprisingly early age, with the first fatty streaking occurring in their arteries before age two. Distressing? Yes. Food for thought? Very much so. So where does the balance lie?

Food and Form

With all of this knowledge accumulating with regard to that most basic of all requirements, food, what kind should we be eating and in what form? There is little scientific evidence that raw food is better than cooked food. Certainly, cooked foods have a higher safety factor by virtue of the heating process, which destroys bacteria and other micro organisms, thereby preventing some diseases.

Many of the necessary molecules and enzymes in raw foods may be available to us and absorbed readily from the gastrointestinal tract, but some are lost to our digestive processes. Cooking some foods makes more nutrients available, as in the case of lycopene from tomatoes. Other carotenes are more readily available from cooked foods. The amount of C and B Vitamins is, however, reduced by cooking. Balance can be achieved by cooking at a low heat for as short a time as possible. Not only will this help preserve the nutrient value, but also ensure that the food is safe.

Despite a lot of negative publicity in their early days, microwave ovens are a very safe way to heat food. They will not heat your food above the boiling point of water. This prevents the conversion of carbohydrates into acrylamides and helps prevent conversion of protein into cancer-causing chemicals. Unfortunately, many of these high heat forming chemicals appeal to your taste buds. High heat is bad for all your foods. Avoid it!

Some foods by nature contain hidden problems. Fish, for example, must be carefully chosen. Larger older fish can contain toxins, so to minimize the chance of taking in too much methylmercury cysteine or chloride (dangerous pro-oxidants), choose shorter-lived smaller fishes such as salmon. In fact, it is recommended that children and pregnant women avoid larger saltwater fish like swordfish and tuna altogether.

Vegetarians

True vegetarians avoid all foods of animal origin. Most of our patients with vegetarian tendencies fall into the category of a somewhat wandering diet that may include fish and those much sought after omega-3 fish oils. Adults must be wary of zinc and Vitamin B12 deficiencies on vegetarian diets. Children are at risk for iron deficiency anemia. Taking extra sources of Vitamin C with vegetable sources of iron (spinach, seeds, nuts, prunes, whole grains and even a little black strap molasses) may increase absorption.

Supplements

Many of us are proponents of appropriate dietary supplementation, particularly when it comes to vitamins, minerals and antioxidants. Soil depletion from intensive agricultural practices over the past 100 years has led to the loss of important trace elements and minerals essential for optimal nutrient content. Although the plant, vegetable or fruit might look wonderful, it could be a poor shadow of the real thing produced from a naturally fertilized nutrient rich soil.

Some scientists feel that credible evidence for supplements does not and will never exist. Unfortunately, good studies are being ignored because belief systems are threatened. 80,000 nurses followed for 14 years showed positive benefits such as a 50 percent reduction in heart disease with no side effects when taking four times the government recommended dose of B6 and folate. Why, then, is not everyone supplemented with these vitamins? A medical school text book I studied stated that vitamin and mineral supplementation was wasteful and unnecessary, shaping many prejudices in student brains. Finally though, the light is beginning to go on and many major western democracies have acknowledged that supplementation may not only be beneficial, but also necessary.

Antioxidants

As we get older, plant-based essentials become even more vital. A major reason for this is that our internal production of important antioxidants like superoxide dismutase, catalase, glutathione peroxidase and alpha lipoic acid all decrease with aging. This is really a double hit – our production of antioxidants is decreasing with time, when we need the protection from antioxidants more than ever as we age. There is no doubt our food is of poorer quality when it comes to its antioxidant potential, particularly vegetables and fruits. As a result of this we must be evermore vigilant when picking our next meal or completing that grocery list.

Proper Fats

We now hear that proper fat ingestion is okay. But what is "proper fat?" Low-fat foods actually increase the amount of carbohydrate intake. A good example is "No fat" sour cream (an oxymoron if ever we heard one), where naturally occurring dairy fat is substituted by Tapioca, a starchy grain. Beware of trans-fat which, when absorbed into the body, will incorporate itself into lipid and protein complexes that do not behave biochemically normal. Abnormal chemistry will lead to abnormal function of the cells and eventually to diseases like hardening of the arteries.

We have stated that natural fats are okay to ingest in moderation, but they must not be oxidized or become rancid, especially by overheating and combining with oxygen. The fats most susceptible to overheating changes are polyunsaturated fats, such as corn, safflower, canola and sunflower oils. Please don't fry or boil these oils. They will become unnatural, unhealthy oxidized oils. If you must heat oil above the boiling point, use a saturated oil (lard) that will not oxidize at those temperatures.

Protecting the Brain

Over the past few decades, we have decreased our intake of dietary omega-3 fats (DHA) by about 80 percent, according to Dr. Donald Rudin, author of *The Omega-3 Phenomenon*. DHA is necessary for metabolically active areas of the nervous system, including the retina, nerve synapse connections, cerebral cortex and nerve mitochondria. DHA comes from cold water fish, marine algae, mildly cooked eggs and mother's milk. Fish is brain food, exactly as your grandmother told you! Here on the West Coast of North America we favor salmon oil but herring, mackerel and a host of small oily fishes will do just as well. The brain is able to make its own DHA from alpha linolenic acid, found in flax seed oil, hemp oil and walnuts.

Literature is full of studies indicating the benefits of multivitamins for the brain. Antioxidant protection of the brain is vital to prevent the fatty brain from literally "going rancid." Many supplements like Ginkgo, green tea, garlic, blueberries and broccoli are showing promise. So start eating fish with a few eggs and some flax seed, finishing off with a dish of blueberries and you are well on the way to protecting your most valuable asset – your brain!

Protecting the Heart

Another vital organ for longevity is the heart. Diet and exercise are key to maintaining a healthy heart. In a study released by the American Heart Association in 2002, there was an astounding 45 percent decrease in death from heart disease in previous heart attack patients if supplemented with those fish oils we mentioned earlier. We know that diets that reduce LDL cholesterol improve cardiovascular health. Eating fish decreased the incidence of heart disease in the ongoing "Nurse's Health Study." Folic acid and B Vitamins have dramatically reduced risk factors for cardiovascular disease. Folate is found in broccoli, whole grains and dairy products.

Stroke

2,000 patients over 40 years old from rural Japan were studied for 20 years. Stroke risk was 70 percent higher in the group with the lowest serum levels of Vitamin C. Those who ate vegetables daily had a 58 percent lower risk of stroke compared to those who ate vegetables only twice per week. *The Journal of The American Medical Association* reported a study showing 75,000 middle-aged women had 43 percent less strokes if they ate at least 2.7 servings of whole grain foods daily. A recent study also showed that 250 mgs of Vitamin C daily could be as effective as some highly touted (and expensive) blood pressure lowering medications. Always work in conjunction with your health care professional on your blood pressure.

Cancer

A high fat diet is implicated as a risk for colon and breast cancer. Processed meats (such as luncheon or smoked) may increase the rate of colon cancer and stomach cancers. Lycopene from tomatoes, selenium from sea food, whole grains and zinc lower the incidence of prostate cancer. Antioxidants from a wide variety of fruits and vegetables point to improved resistance to cancer.

Hormones

There is a significant decline of several important hormones as we get older. Human Growth Hormone (HGH) levels drop after the age of 25 years. The sex hormones, estrogen and progesterone in women and testosterone in men, decline in menopause and andropause. In the past 20 years, it has been realized that HGH is fundamental to adults not only for growth but also for cellular regeneration and repair. There is now a well recognized Adult Growth Hormone Deficiency Syndrome, characterized by loss of muscle mass, additional fat, fatigue and cognitive decline that can be corrected by increasing growth hormone levels. In our "www.healthandlongevitycentre.com" we find that we can optimize cellular regeneration and repair and therefore the health of the individual with a combination of good nutrition and a high quality secretagogue that naturally encourages the release of growth hormone from the pituitary gland. We also balance the other hormones that decline as naturally as possible using bio-identical forms of estrogen, progesterone and testosterone. Results are improvements in energy, enthusiasm, mood, sexual function, body habitus and general well being. Great nutrition with maximal vitamin and antioxidant potential and cells ready and able to optimize that nutrition is the best of both worlds.

So where does all of this leave us? There is lots of good news as so many foods that are good for us are tasty and readily available. We believe we intrinsically have an awareness of those things that are good for us (hence the spiritual and ceremonial aspects of food mentioned), but have drifted away as a result of paying homage to that deity called convenience that controls so much of our busy modern lives. We have therefore lost, to a large extent, the ability to discern. The good news is, that ability soon returns.

Our final words to you are: go for a great diet full of antioxidant protection, relatively low in carbs and with plenty of first class protein and carefully chosen fats. Do enjoyable exercise most days of the week to approach an ideal program to maintain your muscle mass. If you are over 40, look at those hormones that start to decline as we age. Not only will you be avoiding the pitfalls of artery clogging, degenerative diseases and diabetes, but you will be well on the way to your own anti-aging program as well. Bon Chance!

Dr. Donald M. McLeod, M.D., a lecturer and Canadian graduate in medicine, has been in clinical practice for close to 25 years with a special interest in longevity medicine. Dr. McLeod also has a strong interest in astronomy, hockey (coaching, playing and team doctor), is a Pipe Major and a member of A4M, CLA4 and the Canadian Andropause Society. He is the author of *Doctors' Secrets - The Road to Longevity; Doctors' Secrets - The Miracle of Antioxidants; and Doctors' Secrets - Testosterone Power.*
For Anti-aging contact:
Health and Longevity Centre.com
Kelowna, B.C. Canada
250-764-4707

Dr. Philip A. White, M.B., a UK graduate, has been in clinical practice for more than 30 years, as well as spending many years in medical administration. An internationally known lecturer in health care economics and longevity, Dr. White is also an experienced pilot, avid squash player and a member of A4M, CLA4 and the Canadian Andropause Society.

The "Forgotten Link"

By JC Colvin

While health-related infomercial gimmicks make more millionaires on this continent than weekly lottery winners, the average person's belly in North America still resembles the likeness of a spare tire more than a wash board. Fitness is the craze of today's baby boomers (America's largest population surge), but unfortunately, due to video games and modern-day mechanical devices, their offspring and grandkids alike are in worse shape than in any other generation and time in history. How can that be? Today's labor- and time-saving technology has created an overstressed, overworked, overweight and unfit population.

This chapter has been designed for the reader to understand:

1. The benefits and characteristics of the Core Muscle Group in the body and the importance for them to not just look good but to work as a team when called upon.

2. Where core training fits in with a properly designed overall health plan.

3. Specific exercises and recommended "toys" to obtain for effective results from your training.

Power Generator

Stabilization of the body is the process that begins the generation of power that spreads out to the limbs, joints and muscles that require strength for movement. Whether you are going to run, jump, throw, or spit, your core is the birthplace of any and all power supply. Core muscles need be trained with isolation – spinal flexion, extension, lateral flexion and rotation. *Functional Exercises* also need to be incorporated, which require the trunk muscles to synchronize (work together for the activation of a specific movement), resulting in the stabilization of pelvic and spinal position. Power is generated to the rest of the body from this powerhouse by building or coiling up a force, like a spring, while maintaining spinal and pelvic position. While the rest of the body is in motion the power is then uncoiled, creating an explosive muscular force towards the calling muscle/joint/tendon group.

Globally it is accepted that "any object is only as strong as its weakest link." Our population today has one common weak or Forgotten Link – the core. This area of the body's (Rectus Abdominsis, External Obliques, Serratus Anterior and Psoas Group) primary function is not to pull your pelvis and your ribcage together (sorry crunch and infomercial gimmick junkies – close your eyes), but to provide a stable platform from which the other muscles pull.

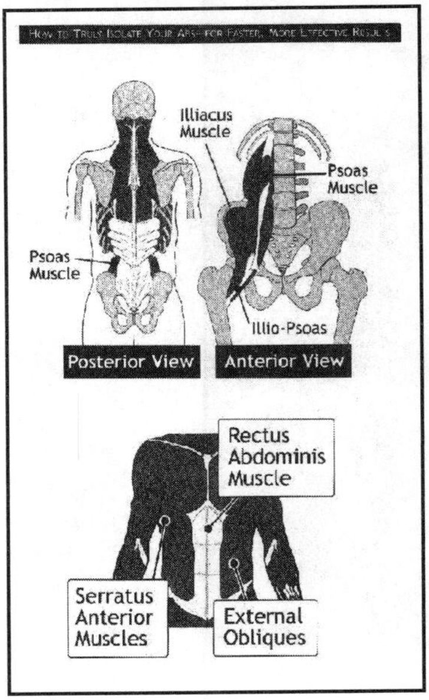

Figure 1

Don't Judge the Book by its Cover

James Garrick, M.D., medical advisor to the National Football League, U.S Figure Skating Team and the San Francisco Ballet, tested the abdominal strength of the U.S. Junior National Gymnastics Team, whose muscle definition he described as "straining belief." His surprising findings were that none of the athletes (a number of whom went on to represent the United States in the upcoming summer Olympics) were able to do five crunches. "It wasn't that they didn't have muscles...it was just that the muscles weren't functioning as a synchronized team. They were doing other things, when they were called into play...they weren't equal to the job," he wrote.

The early 1980's brought the explosion of bodybuilding and, unfortunately, the decline of effective strength training. The size of the muscle was mentally and visually equated to being strong. Hollywood Muscles – all show and no go – were the result, discouraging women from strength training for fear of getting bulky and pushing athletes who needed to maintain certain (low) body weights for competing toward unsafe eating disorders. It has now become widely accepted that bodybuilding was the worst thing that could happen to strength training.

The real reason people train, whether they know it consciously or not, is to gain more energy. Tony Robbins calls it "Unlimited Power!!" Acting as if that is true, then we need to realize that on the other end of the scale, the ultimate lack of energy = DEATH. More energy provides choices. We can consciously choose to, rather than being forced to, participate in activities we enjoy, and more importantly not be all beat up and broken down at the event's conclusion. *Periodization Training* (manipulating the volume of work and intensity of effort in order to achieve a peaking of the body's ability to perform at its best at a specific date in time) is crucial to an efficient work out or energy building program. Placing components of rest, maintenance and recovery phases into the overall plan is critical for optimum results regardless of the level of trainee. Below you can study my designed Energy Pyramid which synchronizes the construction of a complete and harmonious long term body equilibrium package, including *Physical, Emotional and Spiritual* well-being.

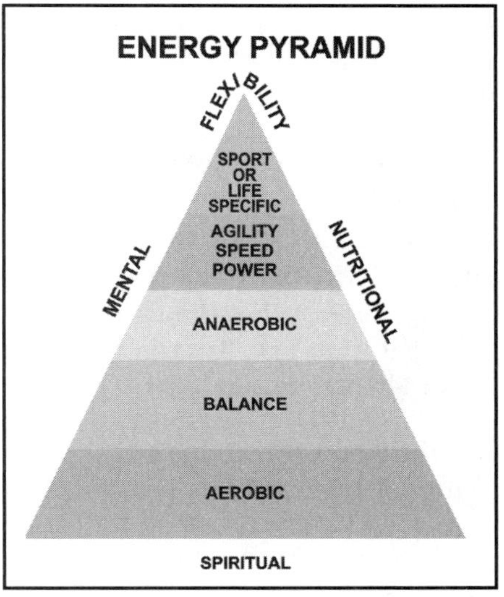

Figure 2

From Figure 2, you can see that there is a time within the Energy Triangle (periodized training year) to train with heavier resistance or weights at 85-90 percent of one's maximum strength. However, my experience of working with high performance athletes (NHL's Vancouver Canucks, University of Denver varsity teams, British Columbia's Free Style Team, and other high level athletes from various sports) has proven time and time over that we can produce much more functional results from training with weights under 20 lbs, using specific patterns and training "toys" throughout the majority of the cyclic year.

My intention here is to explain how strength training your core, The Forgotten Link, will increase your ability to squeeze more horsepower out of the body with better effective techniques. The final results will be a considerable increase in overall strength and functional movement. These techniques can be adapted into any level of training, and will help – for those of us who wish to do so – keep body weight down (women or athletes in sports where bodyweight is a concern). A training program like this also allows body builders and power lifters an ability to "walk the talk" with functional strength and mobility throughout various planes of motion.

Tension = Force

Tension and force are essentially the same thing, which is why bulk free strength training can be defined as acquiring the skills to generate more tension. The more tense your muscles are, the more strength you display - evident in a gymnast's appearance of compact, rock-hard deltoids when performing a crucifix on the rings. In order to obtain this super power and show off your head-turning six pack definition, we must maximize our muscular strength in training. High-tension training relies on four key principals:

1. Slow exercise performance

2. Maximizing muscular tension regardless of the weight being used
3. Minimizing fatigue
4. Taking advantage of various neurological advances (mindset)

Tensing your muscles, as if you were squeezing a piece of coal into a diamond, teaches your body to maximize your muscular tension - the more tense your muscles, the stronger you will get without adding bulk. This tension complies with one of the fundamental laws of physiology: *The Law of Irradiation*, which dictates that the contraction of a muscle will set off a contraction of adjacent muscles, "irradiating" from the muscle directly responsible for the task to its neighbors.

While accepting this solution, let's look at why training our core with common crunches or sit-ups is problematic.

Most people when performing a sit-up literally pull themselves up by their lumbar spine or lower back, which can lead to back problems and/or aggravate existing ones. Crunches pull your rib cage and pelvis together via the abdomen, rounding your back with a forward spinal flexion. The challenge here is that due to our weak North American abdominal muscles, the trainee inevitably does not have the ability to synchronize the stabilizers, resulting in an inability to get the torso off the floor. Therefore they need to rely on the stronger (and tighter) hip flexors to perform the crunch. The inability to round the back with the abs causes the trainee to yank on the spine with the hip flexors to gain momentum. **This results in a dangerous movement for the spine and a useless effort for the abdominal.**

When training the core, or in this case specifically the abdominal, we need to look at isolating the hip flexor with another physiological principal: *The Law of Reciprocal Inhibition.* This law states that a muscle's antagonistic muscle *relaxes* when it contracts, thereby allowing isolation and safe supporting of movements. You can achieve this by placing a spotter's hand under the trainee's calves (Figure 3). While assuming the standard bent knee sit-up/crunch position, the trainee will perform the sit-up/ crunch while steadily pushing against the spotters hands. This pushing effectively activates the knee flexor and hip extensor muscles, relaxing the hip flexors and thus allowing a workout by the abdominal. **This results in no back stress and abdominal isolation.**

Figure 3

Key Principals and Considerations to Fun, Effective Workouts

Most people realize that health and fitness relies largely upon consistent and reasonable effort. While this is true, the thought of adding time and effort into an already bulging time schedule does not exactly motivate or excite us, which is why the almighty "magic pill" is so widely sought after and purchased. Core and balance training workouts can be a FUN, EFFECTIVE and EFFICIENT way of spending our much-limited time. The Excel Development Group's **"No Excuses"** training programs (and living rooms) are designed with an underlying fun atmosphere, with an inexpensive and functional training style.

Good things happen when you are having fun. My Grandfather started walking five miles a day when he was 67, now he is 83 and we have no idea where he is...you get the idea?

Permanently fusing the word *Fun* to the word *Fitness* can be done with the utilization of training "toys" and balance/core exercises. Core training workouts are not only results-orientated and efficient, they can also encourage laughter and play. Training time can be performed with any and all members of the family and in most places (even outside a living room – don't tell my wife, though), thus leaving only two measly excuses for not being in some sort of reasonable shape – time and effort. I write measly because both excuses, more often than not, can be eliminated as these exercises can be performed any time, any place: while on the road, sitting during a family function or even while watching your favorite episode of Will and Grace or finding out who's getting voted off of Survivor.

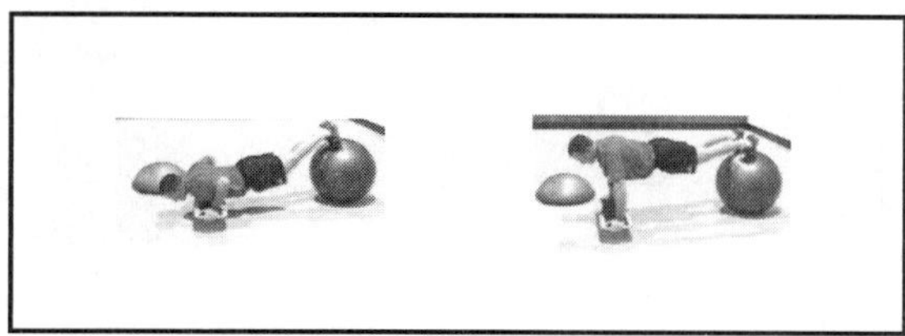

Figure 4

Play is fun – just ask any kid – and something you not only **want** to do but will enjoy doing long term. It's something that you will return to time and time again. It can be challenging or even hard. Figures 4 & 5 show different types of balance or core playing exercises, along with great workout "Toys" that when properly placed into the devised periodized training plan can work wonders for your overall health.

Figure 5

As always, technique is of the utmost of importance and, as with any exercise, one should only perform them while under the supervision of a trained professional and with the consent of a doctor. The Excel Sports Development Group designs and offers integrated periodized training programs. These programs take into account the overall training components, including specific time-sensitive goals, the energy systems of the body, rest, maintenance and recovery, while placing them into phases for an overall plan that is critical for optimizing results or goals, regardless of the level of trainee. The Excel Sports Development Group's training takes movement patterns and balance training exercises and incorporates them into a unique modular training system that helps improve body awareness and balance within every component of fitness, while simultaneously encouraging the aspects of non- and competitive fun and fitness play. Training the "Excel Way" makes you feel good...so do it everyday!!

JC Colvin is a unique individual driven by his calling: Sports Training and Health Development. He has founded his company, The Excel Sports Development Group, on the foundation of Respect, Responsibility, Accountability and Playing Full Out. To learn how to build people, contact JC Colvin by visiting www.excelsportsdevelopment.com.

The E.M.T. Approach:
Giving You the Power to Create and Maintain True Health

By Dr. Richard Baxter

"The doctor of the future will give no medicine but will interest his patients in the care of the human frame, *in diet and in the cause and prevention of disease.*" – Thomas Edison

Many people I meet and most of my patients want their health to improve. These people need to make changes in their lives in order to accomplish this goal. In some cases DRASTIC CHANGES are necessary and in others minor modifications will suffice. Regardless, they all share the same question – "Where do I begin?" Before answering this question we need to define health. The World Health Organization has a fabulous definition stating, "Health is the ability to identify and realize aspirations, to satisfy needs, and to change or cope with the environment. Health is therefore a resource for everyday life, not the objective of living." Wow! Think about that for a moment! Health is something we need to **create and maintain** so that we can realize our potential of living a life of QUALITY as well as quantity.

The power of this information lies not in its originality but in its holism, simplicity and synergy. Much of what is contained here is common knowledge, but rarely is the "big picture" seen together. That is my goal: to present simple unified rules for **creating and maintaining true health.** I will present this information as if we were having a conversation. When I share these ideas in person and guide individuals in making the recommended changes I see amazing results. If you are seeking a positive change in your health I invite you to join in this "conversation" with me.

Recent medical research considers 85-90 percent of all degenerative diseases to be preventable and lifestyle-related. This means that we have an incredible amount of power over our health destiny by choosing to live a health-promoting lifestyle. All it takes is the application of individual responsibility. In order to BE WELL you must *E*at well, *M*ove well and *T*hink well (E.M.T.).

Eating well means eating whole natural food, getting adequate hydration with clean filtered water AND avoiding toxins (this is perhaps the most important point of all when it comes to nutrition).

119

Moving well means performing aerobic AND resistance training, stretching, establishing and maintaining proper posture, and getting proper motion of your spinal joints (extremely important for proper health!)

Thinking well means utilizing positive thinking strategies, setting goals, having a purpose in life and being grateful for those gifts you have been given.

If you examine any fitness or health book on the market it will emphasize one or more of these areas. However none, to my knowledge, combines ALL of the above! Virtually every form of health-promoting activity will fit into one of my three simple categories. Some will combine two. For example, t'ai chi and yoga are forms of movement that also create harmony within your mind and therefore satisfy both moving well and thinking well. One crucial health-promoting activity that does not fit into one of my categories is getting adequate sleep. This is essential to good health and without it none of the other activities are of much use. It forms the key central component of any well-designed health strategy.

You might be skeptical. How can these simple steps make a difference in a world where we have so much technology at our disposal? I have seen time and time again the power of incorporating simple consistent changes into one's life. You don't have to do all of these changes at once but you MUST address each area at some point. A chain with only one weak link is still a weak chain. As with anything in life the more you put in the more you get out. Most people quickly notice some measurable improvement such as a clearer complexion, better sleep, improved body shape, or increased vitality. So read these recommendations with an open mind and open heart, and buckle up because as one patient of mine noted, "this wellness trip is a pretty cool ride."

Eating Well

Too many people are suffering from a basic misunderstanding of nutrition and how their bodies work. Eating to be healthy is not the same as dieting. Nutritional information changes rapidly and today's popular diets often become tomorrow's examples of exactly what *NOT* to do. The best way to avoid being a victim of a passing fad is to apply the laws of human physiology. We need to eat a certain amount of food each day to provide ourselves with enough energy to survive. Within that food there must be certain amino acids, fatty acids, minerals and vitamins. These are called essential components because we cannot make them on our own. The exact dietary requirements for each person could take an entire book so I won't attempt to do that here.

My recommendation is to concentrate on consuming high quality nutrient-dense food and achieving proper hydration. Do not avoid fat altogether but shift from saturated or modified fats to the proper essential fatty acids. Focus on high quality proteins and limit your intake of refined carbohydrates, which can be a source of empty calories leading to high blood-sugar levels. This dietary preference has led to the current North American epidemic of obesity and adult-onset diabetes. Try to get most of your carbohydrates from organic fruits and vegetables. There is some debate as to whether organic food provides more nutrients than non-organic food. Regardless of the outcome of this debate studies have shown that organic produce has, on average, one-third of the amount of pesticide and fertilizer residue. This takes on vital significance considering that avoiding toxins is at least as important as getting adequate nutrition. If you are in North America it is likely that you are not in danger of starving but you might be slowly poisoning yourself. Take the time to read food labels and avoid any products that are highly refined or contain too many ingredients that sound more like chemicals than food. If you can't pronounce it, your body probably can't digest it!

Moving Well

In terms of conventional exercise suffice it to say that strength training is needed to create strong muscles and bones, aerobic exercise is needed to maintain healthy circulation and stretching is required to keep your muscles and joints functioning properly. These forms of exercise also have a multitude of other benefits. Studies have shown that exercise outperforms drugs in fighting depression, reducing stress, losing weight and managing cholesterol levels. Exercise also causes the body to secrete growth hormone, which is responsible for slowing the aging process. So get up and move your body! If you are uncertain, find a qualified professional to get you started on the appropriate exercise regimen.

My remaining recommendations deal with two under-emphasized and misunderstood areas: posture and spinal motion. First let's look at posture. If I ask a group to show me how they would sit if they were depressed, the slumped head and slouched shoulders are very predictable and universal. If I ask the same group to model an Olympic athlete waiting to receive the gold medal the result is also universal, with head held high and chest out. Just by adopting these postures you can feel what I am talking about. We are neurologically programmed to reflect our emotions via posture and the reverse is also true. Poor posture can lead to altered emotions and accelerated wear and tear on the body. However, correcting posture is more than just sitting up straight. It requires a thorough analysis and methods of correction incorporating both physical and neurological means. One of the most effective methods I know is the use of Chiropractic Biophysics™, a technique that was developed by chiropractors and engineers.

Finally we need to examine the importance of proper spinal motion. Chiropractors have always advocated the benefits of keeping the joints of the spine moving properly. Unscientific and uninformed critics have stated that the effect is largely placebo. Modern studies in neuroscience are now providing enough scientific evidence that continued criticism must be considered ignorant and/or malicious. This evidence is so powerful that it has the potential to completely change the modern health paradigm. Perhaps the most profound implication is in the area of stress reduction. Science has shown that stress causes, or significantly contributes to, all of the leading killers such as heart disease, cancer, diabetes and depression. Recent research from Australia is demonstrating that the chiropractic adjustment lowers cortisol levels! Cortisol is the leading hormonal indicator of stress. It also causes accelerated aging and weight gain. So chiropractic adjustments have the potential to lower stress, reduce the incidence of disease, slow aging and help individuals lose weight. In the process some of the other positive effects include reduced pain, relaxed muscles, improved coordination, increased immune function and better moods. Not bad for something that is completely natural! Please be good to your spine and seek out a chiropractor.

Thinking Well

This is an area of particular interest to me. I am fascinated by how two people can experience the same event and one person will consider it to be positive and the other will consider it to be the exact opposite. The explanation lies in what these two people focus on. Viktor Frankl taught us that we can find meaning through suffering even at a level as horrific as the concentration camps. Maxwell Maltz stated that the subconscious mind cannot differentiate between a real experience and one vividly imagined. So while we cannot always choose our experiences, we CAN choose our subsequent repeated thoughts and therefore our feelings. One of the most effective strategies I have learned is the use of questions. Instead of asking "why does this always happen to me?" Try asking positive questions such as "what am I meant to learn from this experience?"

If practiced repeatedly the use of these types of questions will create feelings of positive expectancy and adventure in your life. Seek also to find a purpose to your life. Take the time to examine what fills you with passion and be brave enough to act upon it, if not fully, at least in some capacity. Write out your goals in a positive, present-time format and review them on a regular basis; daily if possible. Seek what you want versus avoiding what you don't. Adopt some form of meditation to quiet your mind each day. You will find that the best answers come from within. One last point on thoughts; be very careful with the words "I am." These are two of the most powerful words in the English language and form a present-time affirmation. Whatever follows those words you will become if you say it frequently enough. So if you say, "I am sorry" many times during the day, you will become "sorry." Far better to say, "I apologize." The good news is that you can use this to your advantage. Just for fun spend the next seven days repeating positive statements using the prefix "I am." Pay attention to the results you get!

The Final Word

The E.M.T. approach is a simple and holistic approach to creating and maintaining true health. To achieve success, every action you take must go through the E.M.T. filter. Ask yourself, "Is this something that qualifies as Eating well, Moving well or Thinking well?" If the answer is YES then you are on your way to improved health. If not, make a choice to change your actions. My hope is that I have stimulated you to think differently about your responsibility for your own health and the power you have in creating it. Begin your journey today; use E.M.T. and BE WELL!

> *"When Health is absent*
> *Wisdom cannot reveal itself*
> *Art cannot become manifest*
> *Strength cannot be exerted*
> *Wealth is useless and*
> *Reason is powerless."*
> – Herophiles, 300 B.C.

Dr. Richard Baxter is a chiropractor and wellness expert practicing in Victoria, British Columbia. His passion is for discovering simple health-enhancing strategies and sharing them through public speaking or written articles. He can be reached at wellness4u@coastnet.com or 250-386-9355.

Eat to Beat Stress

By Dr. Marilyn Joyce, R.D.

Everywhere we look there is another article on stress and how to beat it, or at least how to manage it! Not for one minute would I presume to suggest that all you have to do is eat right and you will eliminate stress. But let's stop for a moment and think about this.

Where do most people eat today? What do they eat? When do they eat? And how do they eat? Let me answer these questions for you.

Where do most people eat today? People generally eat at fast food restaurants or in their car after they have stopped to buy food at a drive thru. Maybe they ordered in (to their home) some fast food and they are eating it in front of the 6:00 p.m. news. Yikes! Just great for their digestion!

What do people eat? Well, let's see. Pizza, hamburgers and fries, so-called health drinks made with sugar-loaded flavored syrups, chicken nuggets, onion rings, batter-covered, deep-fried anything, nitrite-laden deli-cuts in pasty-white rolls. If their intentions are fairly good, maybe they will have an iceberg lettuce (least nutritious lettuce on the face of the earth) salad loaded with death-in-a-bottle – commercial salad dressing! Then there's candy bars and sodas, cookies, donuts, and chips – all of which are loaded with trans fats, salt or sugar or both, and lots of total fat.

When do people eat? Basically most of us eat on the run, in a hurry, gobbling food down between back-to-back meetings. Or we race to pick up the kids from school and get them fed before racing out to an evening meeting or a class of some sort, either for you or for them. Worse – we park ourselves in front of the world news on television, after an already stressful day, and mindlessly eat our fast food as we get more stressed out discovering how seemingly bad the economy is, or that the war on terrorism is escalating. And then we wonder why we have such terrible indigestion!

How do people eat? Well, let me count the ways. In a hurry, on the run, in the car. We eat while talking on the telephone or in front of the television set. We eat at our desk while trying to reach a deadline. We gobble unconsciously just to fill a hole! We wash the food down with gallons of soda! Most of us are unconscious of what we are putting into our mouths, how fast we are eating – or rather inhaling – our food, how tense our bodies are while we are eating, or how we are feeling emotionally as we stuff ourselves. Chewing food is the first step in the digestive process. If we skip this step – well, we all know the outcome! Gas, heartburn, indigestion, just for starters! Obesity, diabetes, cardio-vascular disease, kidney disorders – need I go on?

Beat Stress Before It Beats You

Let me just assure you that I am no stranger to stress myself. I come from the era of the super woman – being all things to all people – and as a type A personality, it all had to be done perfectly. There was no room for error. I raised 2 children as a sole provider, worked more than full time, attended university full time, and was a yoga devotee and teacher to boot – all at the same time! After completing university, I was immediately immersed in an administrative position, which required very long hours, doing a job I hated! And then I developed my own business doing more of this work that I hated – because I was great at doing it (the perfectionist in me) and the money was excellent. I had two teenage kids, a mortgage, and all the fixings of success after the long haul of school and studies. And money, as some of you might remember, was a marker in the 80's of your success, was it not?

Because I was a dietitian, and vegan vegetarian as well (no animal products at all), I thought I was doing everything right. However, I was continually meeting ridiculous deadlines, eating in hospital cafeterias – need I say more on that? – gobbling down food at my desk between meetings and trainings for my staff, or eating in the car on the way to and from work at ungodly hours of the morning and night. I was always worried about my teenage children (anyone with teenagers in the house knows whereof I speak!) while I was working the long hours. I was continually uptight about the endless deadlines and piles of work to be completed that never seemed to diminish in size. There was constant tension between the chef and myself at the various hospitals I worked in, as most of them perceived me to be destroying their creative edge with my demands for healthy meals for the patients. I had no time to think about what was going into my mouth or how complete or incomplete it may have been nutritionally. And exercise and personal self-care were not on my completely overloaded agenda!

In other words, I had no outlet for the chronic stress I was experiencing. So what was happening to my body? The same things that happen to everyone's body in our society today! All the stress we experience has a negative impact on our body, whether it be an argument with our spouse, our kids, our employer, or a friend, being stuck in a serious traffic jam when we are already stretched to the max to get to an important meeting on time (anyone who lives in a city knows this story). Maybe a cutback in staff and overwork at our workplace is cause for major concern due to the necessity of our paycheck for survival. The result is a flooding of the body with little unstable molecules called free radicals. A few will never hurt anyone – just a natural part of living. A lot of these little molecules throughout the body leads to degenerative illness.

And what do we eat when we are under stress? Generally not much that will do a body good! All of those fast food meals and snacks that are so readily available do nothing to fend off the production of free radicals. They are generally devoid of the multitude of vitamins, minerals, antioxidants, phytochemicals (plant chemicals), bioflavonoids, fiber, and the myriad of yet to be discovered nutrients found in foods that come from the farm! No metabolic function can occur in our body without all of these thousands of nutrients working together synergistically. Energy production occurs when these nutrients connect and work together with water and oxygen in the mitochondria, which is the energy production factory, in *every* cell in the body. (Yes, you need to drink that 6 – 8 glasses of water you keep hearing about and get yourself into a yoga class or some other form of exercise where you learn to breathe deeply if you want to have energy.) If just one piece of this puzzle is missing, we are in deep doodoo!

The price I paid for not dealing effectively with my stress was very high! At 35 years of age I was diagnosed with terminal cancer and spent the following 5+ years fighting for my life. In 1989, I found myself weighing 88 pounds, in a wheelchair, unable to hold anything down – food or water (liquids in general!). Over those years I learned a tremendous amount about what to do and what not to do, what to eat and what to avoid, what I could eat (hold down), and what was simply not going to get past my lips. From sucking on only ice chips in 1989 to a diet of wonderful whole foods as close as possible to the way they came from the farm, I had to go through a lot of lessons and a lot of changes in my life and attitude in order to regain and maintain optimum health. Returning from that "Dark Night of the Soul" to great health taught me the ultimate truth – that *health is the only true wealth!* Without it, nothing else is possible. With it, the sky is the limit – anything is possible! *I had to beat stress before stress beat me.* And the first big step started with what I passed through my lips – the foods that contained the natural elements necessary to keep this precious engine running with optimum precision.

Better Choices...

In my work over the years with chronically ill clients – cancer, MS, fibromyalgia, heart disease, and other degenerative illnesses – chronic fatigue has been a predominant complaint. Almost across the board, within a short space of time, with the addition of a good supply of pure water, the elimination of most fast foods and commercial snack foods, the addition of wholesome vegetables and fruits, some whole grains (brown rice, quinoa, buckwheat, millet, etc., not commercially packaged foods and breads masquerading as whole grains) and about 30 minutes of exercise five times a week, this condition of fatigue is significantly reduced. Why? Because the nutrients and other elements necessary for energy production are being provided.

In turn, when the body has sufficient energy being produced, the thousands of other metabolic functions, which depend on this energy supply for their own ability to function, are able to do their respective jobs. Therefore, not only is the fatigue reduced or eliminated, but the body's ability to handle stress effectively is positively increased. The body's antidote to free radicals is the inclusion of all of those nutrients listed earlier! And where do you get them? From foods that came to you directly from the farm without a stop at a factory along the way (such as the foods listed in the chart below)!

Does it take a lot of time? NO! Does it take a lot of money? NO! Does it take a lot of thought? NO! *Just better choices!* Most importantly, make it fun. And be as passionate about your health and improved ability to handle stress as you are about all of those material goals and dreams that you are working on. Take it from me: without your health, nothing – and I mean nothing! – else matters!

Recommendations for Your Journey to Optimum Health

Instead of:	*Use:*
Candy, Cookies	Fresh fruit, applesauce, dried fruits (3 – 5 servings per day)
Battered fried veggies	Fresh, raw or lightly steamed vegetables, fresh raw salads with homemade dressings, raw veggie sticks with healthy bean or vegetable dips (5 – 9 servings per day)
Roasted salted nuts	Raw almonds, cashews, brazil nuts (handful only)
Roasted salted seeds	Raw sesame, sunflower, and pumpkin seeds
Commercial nut butters, i.e. peanut butters	Fresh ground almond, cashew or sesame seed butters (Sesame tahini is ground sesame seed spread)
Hydrogenated plant oils & or Canola oil	Pure virgin olive oil, expeller pressed sesame oil; expeller pressed walnut, flaxseed, almond, safflower oils
White, distilled vinegar	Balsamic, rice, wine vinegars
Ground round (beef)	Ground turkey breast, ground buffalo meat: limit red meats, especially beef, to 2X / mo, and only organic, hormone- and antibiotic-free
Regular whole grain breads	Sprouted whole grain breads & bagels

Mayonnaise of any sort	Nonfat plain yogurt, organic, Vegenaise, Soyanaise
Soyannaise, Vegenaise, etc.	Nonfat or low fat plain yogurt, organic
Commercial salad dressings	Homemade dressings
Regular pasta	Whole wheat or other whole grain pasta (2X week)
Regular grocery store eggs	Cage-free, free range, fertilized eggs
Regular grocery store yogurt	Organic, hormone-free, low fat or fat-free yogurt
Beef Burgers	Turkey Burgers (made from ground turkey breast), Garden or Boca Burgers (organic or no GMO's)
Sugary sodas, fruit-flavored drinks	Sparkling water or club soda with fresh lemon or lime, low-sodium vegetable or tomato juice

Dr. Marilyn Joyce, R.D. is an internationally acclaimed inspirational speaker, writer, radio and television personality, and one of the world's leading authorities on nutrition and lifestyle for the prevention and overcoming of cancer and other degenerative illnesses. Her lively, information-packed seminars and workshops are loaded with powerful, proven strategies for creation of outstanding health and vitality. Dr. Joyce is the author of *"5 Minutes to Health"* and *"I Can't Believe It's Tofu!"*
Check out: **www.marilynjoyce.com** and sign up for her free e-letter, or call **(800) 352-3443.**

Why You Shouldn't Have To Suffer With Pain

By Dr. Rick Swartzburg, D.C.

A fire alarm goes off in a building. Within moments, the diligent fire department arrives on the scene and immediately turns off the alarm. With that done, the fire fighters all go back to the station, never even checking to see what caused the alarm to go off.

Sound a little ridiculous? While this scenario is definitely not how the fire department reacts to a fire, it still amazes me that this is how most people react to a more common alarm that frequently goes off...PAIN! Pain is essentially a series of chemically mediated responses that serve much of the same purpose as a fire alarm would...to warn you when something is wrong.

So does this mean that you should never do anything to help eliminate your pain? Absolutely not. But, as with a fire alarm, you definitely shouldn't turn off the alarm until you know for sure that the fire is put out.

When pain is prolonged more than six months it is known as chronic. Chronic pain sufferers can have difficulty functioning with normal physical and emotional tasks. In the United States approximately 120 million people suffer from chronic pain, with an estimated cost exceeding $125 billion annually in health care, disability compensation, lost productivity, and lost tax revenue. With staggering figures like that, it is no wonder the drug industry has a thriving pain relief business.

Some of the more common painful conditions seen are arthritis, carpal tunnel, fibromyalgia, bursitis, tendonitis, sprains, strains, disc herniations, headaches, TMJ disorder, and a whole host of other back, neck, hip, knee, elbow, ankle, foot, wrist, hand, and shoulder conditions. You can also factor in the stress that your body goes through when it is subjected to continual amounts of pain. When pain has become so intense that it does cause stress to your body, this can not only deter proper healing of an area, but has been linked to a variety of conditions and diseases. While all of these disorders are very different in their cause, most doctors have no problem prescribing the same type of pain medications to relieve the patient's symptoms without ever trying to eliminate the cause of their patient's pain.

MENTOR #23

Reducing pain should only be done once you know the reason for your pain. The toxicity of oral medications implicates that it may be more dangerous to use them to eliminate your pain. In 1998, over one hundred thousand prescription drug-related deaths and about two million severe drug-interaction related injuries were reported. The Journal of the American Medical Association reported that adverse drug reactions became the fourth most frequent cause of death. Quite a number of these deaths were from oral medications used to treat painful conditions.

With these frightening statistics, it may turn out that topical pain relievers may hold the best promise for pain relief due to their amazing safety record. Of course, not all topical pain relievers are created equal. A good topical pain reliever will properly penetrate the skin directly over a painful area and contain ingredients that work to alter local chemistry to the area of pain, not just add irritating or numbing medication. The natural ingredients MSM and Glucosamine have been shown in numerous studies to be beneficial for the reduction of tissue inflammation and healing of damaged cartilage material. Use of small molecular sized compounds, such as MSM and Glucosamine, can be used effectively in a topical solution, but only if it is formulated with ingredients that help it slip through the difficult-to-penetrate first layer of skin. Liposomes have been demonstrated to be such ingredients, but only if there are no waxy or oily substances that prevent it from allowing proper skin penetration to occur.

By using the best type of topical pain reliever and working to address the cause of your pain with nutritional supplements, supports, exercises, sleep aids and other forms of therapeutic care, I strongly believe that you shouldn't have to live with pain.

While pain can be a great warning sign that our bodies use as a defense mechanism, **there are very good reasons to eliminate the pain once a cause is discovered.** One very important reason would be to get better sleep. We know that pain can interrupt the normal sleep cycle, either by keeping you up tossing and turning, or just by preventing you from reaching that important last restful Delta phase of sleep. This interruption of sleep has been linked to chronic muscle conditions, such as fibromyalgia, and has been demonstrated to reduce healing of the body for all types of conditions. Research has shown that sleep interruption, especially as a result of working the "graveyard" shift, can increase the risk of developing cancer by up to 60%.

Why Your Mattress May Be the Problem

The connection between poor sleep and conditions such as fibromyalgia and chronic back pain has been well documented, but what people most often forget is that it is not the quantity of sleep that is important, but rather the quality. It is the most important slow-wave sleep (delta-wave) that determines whether your muscles can actually relax and finally shut down. It takes a cycle of three complete sleep phases to allow you to reach this final resting stage of sleep. For fibromyalgia sufferers, the muscles are like a 24-hour convenience store that never stops working.

A 1999 study by the Department of Biobehavioral Nursing and Health Systems, University of Washington, demonstrated that delta-wave sleep deprivation leads to decreased pain threshold, increased discomfort, fatigue, and the inflammatory flare response in skin. This study basically took healthy individuals and created fibromyalgic-like symptoms without even reducing any actual sleep time. While the study used sound to inhibit the delta-wave sleep, a poor mattress can also inhibit this phase of sleep for two reasons. Firstly, improper support from a poor mattress will cause your body to shift frequently throughout the night to find a more comfortable position. Every time you shift your body, you are breaking the sleep cycle and therefore inhibiting the chance of reaching the healing delta phase sleep. Secondly, if your mattress increases pressure to specific muscles and joints of the body, the resulting compression on these areas may cause pain and tenderness. Pain will also lead to a break in the sleep cycle and prevent delta-wave sleep from occurring.

The solution is to use a mattress that conforms to your body and traces the bumps and curves to evenly disperse the mattress pressure throughout your total body. This will allow you to better reach the delta-wave sleep by remaining in a more comfortable and supportive position throughout the night. Higher-grade memory and latex foam will do this, but then return to its normal shape afterwards. Throw out the old spring mattress and don't believe the air mattress hype – they just provide you with an inward bending hammock effect and will not offer the support you need to sleep your way back to health.

Choosing the Correct Mattress and Sleeping Position

A good mattress will protect the back for the many hours that you are in bed. A mattress that properly supports the body will also be a very important element in helping relieve stress on the muscles and joints of the back. The most important information needed for finding a correct mattress to support the back involves knowing what position you sleep in.

A mattress that properly supports the body should be solid enough to not cave inward with body pressure and yet have enough give to allow contouring of the body. This is especially important with side sleepers, as a lot of pressure is placed on the shoulders and hips. Don't be fooled by all those promotions which state that firm mattresses are necessary for good support. Firm mattresses work better for back sleepers than they do for side or stomach

131

sleepers. While back sleepers can get away with a more firm mattress, the contouring of the body that occurs with a mattress that gives when pressure is applied will hold the body in a more proper position for a comfortable sleep. Sleeping on your stomach can be irritating to your neck and back due to the complete rotation of the neck to one side while in this position. To help yourself achieve the best sleep for whatever ever position you are sleeping in, keep the following in mind:

Choose a mattress that feels like it gives enough on the surface to comfortably keep you locked into a supportive position. Memory foam and latex foam will accomplish this most effectively. Memory foam is a pressure-sensitive or temperature-sensitive polyurethane foam that has the ability to compress, then **slowly** come back to its original shape. Therefore, memory foam does not place nearly the same resistance on the joints as springs, air, and other materials that bounce back more rapidly. Memory foam mattresses are usually composed of three inches of the temperature sensitive visco-elastic foam over five inches of regular polyurethane foam. High resiliency polyurethane material makes an ideal supportive base for the mattress. Memory foam is usually found in three to five pound densities. The higher density memory foam, usually five pounds and up, will become softer when it heats up with body temperature and harder with any drop in room temperature. This makes five-pound memory foam more temperature sensitive, heavier, and usually stiffer (especially when the temperature drops at night). Four-pound memory foam is less dense, more soft, and less expensive, but also a little less supportive. Certain types of latex foam will also be soft enough to contour the body, but provide a bit more of a spring effect.

This material can be combined well with memory foam to make up a mattress, but neither substance should be used in the bottom base layer of the mattress. This is because you never want to sink too much into the mattress, causing a folding effect of your body and losing support. For this reason, people who are primarily side sleepers can utilize more of the memory and latex foam. This is due to the fact that the shoulders and hips stick out farther, and therefore need more contouring if you are going to attempt to evenly distribute your weight over the whole of the mattress. People who are primarily back sleepers may need more of a firmer support material underneath the latex and/or memory foam, as less contouring is needed.

While it is not recommended that you sleep on your stomach, if you do, always wedge a pillow under one side of the pelvis and same side leg, thereby limiting the amount of rotation of the upper spine. Back sleepers can place a pillow under their legs to reduce traction on the spine. When lying on your side, always put a pillow or orthopedic leg spacer between your knees to prevent rotation of the pelvis and spine. Leg spacers help prevent torque on the spine from pelvic rotation when you are on your side, while moving with your body if you roll on your back. This measure will combine to keep your spine in a more correct alignment while sleeping. While back sleeping is still the most supportive position for the spine, and stomach sleeping will still have the potential to irritate the muscles and joints, these tips should combine to keep your spine in a more correct alignment, while giving the rest of your body the relief of the kind of weightless sleep you've only dreamed about.

In addition to his ten years of Chiropractic practice,
Dr. Rick Swartzburg, D.C. has authored an informative video on the topic
of headaches, an informational book called "You Don't Have to Live with
Pain" and produced web sites titled the *#1 Back Pain Site* (1backpain.com),
memoryfoammattress.org and Tendonitis.net. These sites offer
the reader instant information about conditions, therapies,
exercises, helpful products, and doctors who treat
various painful conditions. Located in
Thousand Oaks, California, Dr. Swartzburg
maintains a busy practice. He currently
heads up the product development
for **Relief-Mart** (www.reliefmart.com)
and **Selectabed.com,**
where he has helped create and
bring variety of helpful pain relief
and support products to the public.

Save Your Health
with Fats

By Marc St-Onge

Twentieth century technological advances in the agriculture and food processing industries have given us, as the Bible puts it, dominion over the land. Isn't it ironic then that we live in a society where diet-related disease has become epidemic? Where can we place the blame?

Technology? No, certainly not. Technology is only as good as the motivation behind it. Similarly, our health is only as good as our motivation to be healthy. Luckily, we all can achieve good health. That's a matter of fact. How do we achieve good health? Let's view this question from the other side and ask, "How did we ever come to achieve such poor health?"

MENTOR #24

Although we can't blame technology, let's look at the role it has played. With respect to our food supply, it has allowed us to drastically alter our dietary habits. Although humans are very adaptable creatures, we adapt very poorly to changes in our diet. For many millennia, humans have enjoyed a fairly consistent diet which, through evolution, is reflected in our genetic makeup. Staple foods included lots of fish, wild game, free-roaming livestock, and plenty of fruits and vegetables. This ancestral diet came to an abrupt end once we hit the 20th century. The "fast food" revolution pushed the emphasis towards convenience and taste. With this came the onslaught of grain-based, highly refined products. Prepackaged foods that required little preparation and could sit on a shelf for months became the hallmark of the modern diet. And while our radically new diet offered convenience and sensual tastes, it offered little of what's required for health – nutrients. It can be easily argued that a lack of essential nutrients in the diet is one of the greatest contributors to poor health.

Essential nutrients are the building blocks of life and when we deprive ourselves of even just a few nutrients we steer ourselves down the path of poor health. In North America we suffer from multiple nutrient deficiencies and one of the worst deficiencies in our diet is – fat! Yes, a fat deficiency. It is of vital importance that you realize that not all fats are created equal. Some fats are bad, some are okay in moderation, and some are actually a matter of life and death. These vital fats are known as essential fatty acids (EFAs). More specifically, we have two groups of EFAs; omega-3s and omega-6s. EFAs are, as the name says, essential.

Like other essential nutrients, these fats must be provided by our diet since our bodies cannot manufacture them. One of the major differences between EFAs and other fats is that they have a different metabolic fate in the body. Your body prefers not to burn EFAs as an energy source and they are therefore less likely to contribute to body fat stores. Better yet, EFAs are not only unlikely to be stored as body fat, they actually promote weight loss. But this is not wherein lays the power of EFAs. These vitally important fats are used by the body for countless biological functions including cardiovascular function, mental health, immune system regulation, hormonal balance, inflammation control, nerve function, brain function, sexual function, and even for radiant-looking skin and hair.

Stating that the North American population is severely EFA deficient is only a half-truth. The truth is that most of us suffer from an omega-3 deficiency but consume large amounts of omega-6s. Does this present itself as a half-good and half-bad scenario? Actually, it's all bad. In researching EFAs, scientists have identified that we not only require both omega-6s and omega-3s but they must also be present in a ratio of about 1:1. An excess of one will interfere with the role of the other. It's estimated that the omega-6 to omega-3 ratio of a typical diet is about 20:1. Therefore, our deficiency of omega-3 fatty acids is accentuated by the fact that we consume excessive amounts of omega-6s and quite frankly, that spells trouble. Where is all this omega-6 coming from in our diet? Common cooking oils including corn, safflower, soy, sunflower, and sesame are rich in omega-6s. Additionally, chicken fat is high in omega-6s, as are most nuts and seeds. As you can guess, these fats are present in countless prepared and processed foods sitting on store shelves.

What foods are sources of omega-3s? Your choices are somewhat limited in comparison. The best source of omega-3s is fish. Flax seed oil also contains a large percentage of omega-3s but they are unfortunately poorly utilized by the body. So here is the solution: consume plenty of fish and decrease your consumption of all those omega-6 rich foods. Sounds pretty simple, but once again, our health is only as good as our motivation to be healthy. Most people find it extremely difficult to cut back on all those omega-6 rich foods, let alone all the saturated fats and dangerous trans-fats. At the same time, most people aren't willing to consume 4-5 weekly servings of fresh fatty fish such as herring, salmon, and mackerel. To make matters worse, eating certain types of fish comes with its own set of precautions. Our oceans, and consequently our fish supply, have become contaminated with environmental toxins. Fish farming practices have also come into question due to the use of chemically treated feed. Farmed fish are also much lower in omega-3s than their wild counterparts.

Does this mean we shouldn't eat fish? No, this simply means that we should eat certain fish in moderation and opt for fish sources that are from clean waters or are lower on the food chain. The discovery of omega-3 health benefits has led to health food retailers lining their shelves with omega-3 fish oil supplements. While they do not offer the complete nutritional benefits of eating fish, omega-3 fish oil supplements are an excellent way to make sure you're getting enough of this vital nutrient. If choosing to go the route of supplements to get your omega-3s, always make sure the manufacturer can provide you with lab test results showing the product meets international standards for mercury, dioxins, pesticides, and PCBs.

Now that it's clear that we need to increase our omega-3 consumption, here are the basics of how EFAs work in the body. EFAs are a key component of cellular membranes. Here they play both a structural and functional role by creating membrane stability, facilitating oxygen transfer, and energy production. Omega-3s are extremely vital to the proper functioning of the body's electrical system. For this reason, healthy brain and nerve tissue contain an extremely high concentration of omega-3s. EFAs are also precursors to a class of hormonelike substances called prostaglandins. Prostaglandins regulate vital cellular functions in the body. There are three primary classes of prostaglandins; PG1, PG2, and PG3. Like hormones, when prostaglandins are out of balance they create an unhealthy state in the body. Although all three types are essential for good health, it's generally considered that PG1 and PG3 have a positive effect while PG2 exerts primarily a negative effect. Excessive production of PG2 promotes harmful cardiovascular effects such as increased blood platelet stickiness, clot formation, and elevated blood pressure. PG2 also promotes inflammation in the body that can lead to numerous degenerative and immune system disorders including arthritis, asthma, gastrointestinal disease, cancer, and autoimmune disease. The good PG3 prostaglandins are produced from omega-3s while omega-6s are responsible for the production of both the good PG1 and the bad PG2. Therefore, high omega-6 consumption leads to increased PG2 production and potential for disease. An added benefit of healthy omega-3 levels is that they have the ability to suppress the production of the bad PG2.

With all this talk about omega-3 fatty acids it should be pointed out that the reference is to two particular types; eicosapentaenoic acid (EPA) and docosahexaenoic acid (DHA). These are the two active forms of omega-3s and are responsible for the health benefits. EPA and DHA are the forms naturally present in high concentrations in certain fish. As previously mentioned, flax seeds are a less optimal source of omega-3s. The type of omega-3 present in flax seed oil is called alpha-linolenic acid (ALA). Although your body can convert ALA to EPA and DHA this process is very inefficient. Studies have found this conversion typically results in less than 10 percent of ALA being converted to EPA and DHA. Providing your body with omega-3s in the form of EPA and DHA also frees up special enzymes that assure better conversion of omega-6s to the active forms. Since fish oil is such an excellent source of both EPA and DHA, most omega-3 research focuses on the use of omega-3s derived from fish. With all the functions in the body that rely on omega-3s, its no wonder thousands of studies have demonstrated significant therapeutic benefits for a broad range of conditions and diseases.

Cardiovascular Disease

One of the biggest areas of omega-3 research is cardiovascular disease. Back in the 1970's, researchers were curious as to why the high fat diet (which included saturated fats) of Eskimos in Greenland resulted in such a low incidence of heart disease. It was determined that the cardio-protective effects were the result of their high omega-3 intake. Thousands of studies later, there is clear evidence that the omega-3s EPA and DHA reduce serum triglycerides, raise HDL (good) cholesterol, and reduce platelet aggregation, thus preventing blood clots. They can also improve elasticity of artery walls, stabilize the electrical currents of the heart and support normal blood pressure. The American Heart Association now emphasizes the importance of regular omega-3 consumption for promoting a healthy heart and cardiovascular system.

Depression and Neurological Disorders

The number of cases of depression in North America is on its way to becoming epidemic. Comparatively, populations that consume fish on a regular basis have drastically reduced incidences of depression and neurological disorders. The highest concentrations of the omega-3 DHA are found in the cells of the nervous system. A healthy cerebral cortex contains 20% DHA while the retina of the eye contains up to 60% DHA. Low DHA levels in the brain have been shown to result in lower levels of important brain chemicals such as dopamine, adrenaline, norepinephrine, serotonin, and endorphins. Low levels of these key brain chemicals can manifest as depression, increased pain sensitivity, addictive behavior, anxiety, aggression, dementia, and ADD. Research has also demonstrated an omega-3 connection with bipolar, schizophrenia, and Parkinson's disease.

Arthritis and Inflammation

By suppressing the production of the pro-inflammatory PG2 prostaglandin and stabilizing cell membranes, omega-3s have a direct anti-inflammatory effect in the body. Therefore, omega-3 consumption is effective in the prevention and treatment of conditions such as osteoarthritis and rheumatoid arthritis, eczema, psoriasis, acne, ulcerative colitis, and asthma.

Diabetes

New omega-3 research is also demonstrating an anti-diabetic effect. Omega-3s appear to improve insulin sensitivity in those with type II diabetes. Statistics have shown that a high omega-6 to omega-3 ratio is associated with an increased prevalence of non-insulin dependant diabetes. Diabetes is also a risk factor for cardiovascular disease and neuropathy (nerve damage) making omega-3 intake especially important for diabetics.

Cancer

Cancer has become one of the most exciting areas of omega-3 research. There is clinical evidence suggesting the balance of essential fatty acids plays a significant role in the development, prevention, and treatment of cancer. Statistical data clearly shows a reduced incidence of many types of cancer in people who consume fish on a regular basis. Research has discovered that most cancer cells contain high levels of omega-6s and consequently exhibit an overproduction of the harmful PG2 prostaglandin. Increased production of PG2 appears to be essential for the survival and proliferation of cancer cells. Omega-3s, potent inhibitors of PG2, have demonstrated anti-cancer properties including suppression of tumor growth and inducing cancer cell death. Tumor cell cultures subjected to various omega-6 to omega-3 ratios demonstrated suppression of tumor growth with an equal 1:1 ratio but as the percentage of omega-6s increased, tumor growth was actually stimulated. The high omega-6 to omega-3 ratio of the typical North American diet could therefore be considered a risk factor for the development of cancer.

Luckily, EFA research is gaining momentum throughout the world. It is clear that omega-3s possess a therapeutic benefit in the treatment and control of various diseases. In North America, our biggest problem is not in the treatment of disease, but the prevention of these same diseases. Preventative measures are by far our best way of enjoying a healthy life. Without health we struggle to find happiness. Without happiness we struggle to find hope. Let this be your motivation!

Marc St-Onge, BSc, is a health researcher and motivational speaker. Born and living in Nova Scotia, Marc has developed a lifelong passion for the sea and its many health benefits. Marc is also the president of the award-winning supplement company Ascenta Health Ltd. For more information you can visit www.ascentahealth.com

Building the Body of a Champion

By Joe Loiacano

The key to a healthy life is to know and understand the steps necessary to build the body you desire and deserve, and to understand how they affect your general well being. You must make them a way of life. This is crucial.

– Joe Loiacano

Create a Positive Mental Attitude (PMA)

In your quest for the perfect body, the most vital component is your attitude – what you think is what you get. The old saying "You must believe it to achieve it" certainly holds true when building the perfect body. Here we are talking about the power of internal visualization, which will help immensely to develop a healthy mind, attitude and clear vision of where you want to be. It is the process I use (and have taught many others) of visualizing the body the way you want it to look. First you create it in your mind, then it materializes within time. Set your goals and let nothing stop you! Find details about the "Baseball Diamond Method" on our website at www.FitCoaching.com.

Benefits of Creative Visualization

- Creative visualization works because your subconscious mind does not know what is real and what is fiction. It simply creates your reality based on the image that you visualize.

- Creative visualization is so effective because it relies on what your mind is doing already, producing the internal results you imagine. Why not put into your mind consciously the results you desire by intentionally visualizing what you want, instead of settling for the results you have unconsciously visualized in the past?

Proper Aerobic and Cardiovascular Exercise

Aerobic energy comes from the natural chemical reaction of your cells to increased oxygen. Make every minute in the gym count with the correct cardio respiratory routine. In this process, fats and proteins are broken down, making aerobic workouts ideal for fat loss. Aerobic exercise increases heart rate, strengthening the organ's ability to contract. Stronger contractions mean an improved, stronger blood flow, in turn making a body better equipped for exercise.

Tips for Building Aerobic Endurance

- Maintain your workout for at least 15-30 minutes at your target heart rate.

MENTOR **#25**

139

- If you are having trouble maintaining 30 minute workouts, try staggering three 10 minute shifts throughout the day.

- Workout at least 3-4 times a week for lasting effects.

- Slowly increase your aerobic activities over a period of time to improve performance. Generally the more aerobic demands you make on your body, the stronger it gets. But be moderate. Gradual increases prevent injury.

- Rest. The body needs time to recover and grow. Alternating days and varying the intensity of workouts can aid in your overall development and prevent injury. Pay attention to your body's messages – soreness, tension, aches – so you know when to work and when to rest.

Your cardio respiratory routine should be monitored and changed periodically to keep your body stimulated and moving towards your goals.

Anaerobic energy is different from aerobic. It produces short term bursts of energy, and does not require oxygen. This energy comes from the burning of carbohydrates and is directly responsible for increasing muscular strength. It can be sustained for several minutes, after which a short rest time is needed to replenish the system. Anaerobic energy is used for everything from weight lifting and sprinting to tennis and golf. Anaerobic energy is also used within aerobic-centered workouts when additional spurts of energy are needed.

Increase Muscular Strength

Enhanced muscular strength often increases muscle and connective tissue size and density by enlarging cells, or building muscles. Apart from their aesthetic value, larger muscles and connective tissues are less prone to accidents and aid long term weight control, since muscle tissue burns more calories than fat, even while resting.

Tips for Building Muscular Strength

- Stagger exercises. Concentrate on activities that work specific muscle groups. Work slowly with concentration on form and resistance to gravity.

- Anaerobic activity produces lactic acid build-up in muscle tissue, which can be temporarily painful. Stretching before and after workouts prevents this condition.

- Like aerobic workouts, gradual progression of stress on muscles will increase muscular strength.

- A warm-up is crucial to any workout.

- Rest. One or two day's recovery time is necessary for maximum effect and injury prevention.

Increase Muscular Endurance

Muscle endurance is the measure of how well muscles can repeatedly generate force, and the amount of time they can maintain activity. Muscular endurance is the practical use of raw strength. It is crucial for every fitness activity, from the mostly anaerobic weight lifting repetitions also known as "reps," to intense aerobic activities like jogging (where specific muscles in the legs are used repeatedly). Muscular endurance combines both aerobic and anaerobic energy.

Tips for Building Muscular Endurance

- Like aerobic endurance and muscular strength, muscular endurance is increased through overload. Overworking the muscles makes them stronger and gives them more endurance. But don't overdo it. Moderate increases achieve the same result with lower risk of injury.

- When weight lifting, averaging three sets of 10-12 lift repetitions is an excellent way to build endurance.

- Rest between workouts.

Food Intake

Proper nutrition is one of the most common obstacles to achieving your ideal body. If your goal is to improve your appearance, exercise alone won't do it. Do you know how many calories and what percentages of carbohydrates, proteins and fats you need to reach your fitness goals?

Four hours or more without eating slows down the metabolism. Then the hunger causes you to eat everything in sight. This is usually at night, so the food consumed before sleep turns into fat.

Tips for Proper Food Intake

- Eat moderate meals every two to three hours.

- You must burn more calories than you take in.

- Remember, scale weight is not a reliable indication of what is really happening.

Supplementation

Supplements are, without a doubt, one of the most important aspects of an athlete's arsenal. It is perfectly fine to have an amazing workout routine, but if your diet and supplement routines fail, your results will be compromised. Supplements are the difference between good results, and great results. They provide your body with the nutrients needed to reach your goals without adding calories.

Tips for Supplementation

- Use supplements wisely, not as a crutch. Never think for a minute that any pill is going to take the place of dedication and willpower. Diet comes first.

141

- When constructing a supplement program, give attention to the careful selection of a multi-vitamin.

- Obtaining enough protein in the diet alone is often difficult. That is why I recommend a good whey protein.

- Creatine is an excellent supplement that when used as part of a strength program. It can produce great gains in lean muscle tissue for the user.

- Glutamine is important because the body is unable to make enough of it on its own when subject to intense and training. Without an external supply of glutamine gains will be minimized.

- When on a fat-loss program, a thermogenic can greatly increase fat loss. Two popular brands are Hydroxycut and Xenadrine.

Increase Your Flexibility

Flexibility is the ability to stretch your muscles and the tendons and ligaments that connect them to your bones. You increase flexibility by stretching the elastic fibers beyond their usual limits and maintaining that stretch for a few moments. The fibers will eventually adjust to these new limits.

Increased flexibility decreases the risk of injury while exercising, and increases your exercise performance. Certain activities, such as swimming and yoga, require greater flexibility than others.

Tips for Increasing Flexibility

- Stretch before a workout, but after warming up. Warmed-up muscles will be more limber, and less at risk for rips or pulls.

- Stretching after a workout helps relax strained muscles and prevent cramping.

- Stretching should never be painful. Stretch gently so you feel it, but not so much that you feel it hurt.

- Keep constant tension on your muscles, tendons and ligaments – don't bounce.

- Stagger stretching specific body areas throughout the day.

- For maximum results, stretch regularly - several times a day, at least five days a week.

Be Patient

You didn't put that ring around your belly on in one day, and you won't take it off in one day either. Don't get discouraged. Burning just a little bit of fat every day will add up over the weeks and months. In today's world we want everything right this second, but you can't rush dieting unless you want to end up losing all your muscle and looking and feeling sickly and weak.

You'll get there if you keep doing the right things...just be patient.

Tips for Patience

The Baseball Diamond Method at www.fitcoaching.com has been specifically designed to increase your patience.

Hire a Fitness Coach

A fitness coach (FitCoach) is similar to a personal trainer. However, a personal trainer trains you in the gym. This limits your selection to people available locally. A "FitCoach" does similar work, but the training is done on the phone during your scheduled weekly coaching call, through tele-seminars, and Web training.

All FitCoaches are carefully selected and are fully certified. Many have degrees in the field, years of experience as a certified personal trainer, and a great track record.

Benefits of Hiring a FitCoach

- Access to some of the best trainers in the country. You don't have to settle for local run of the mill trainers.

- Develop a personalized training program customized for you.

- Your food intake, cardio exercise, resistance exercise and supplement recommendations are monitored and modified to reach your individual goals

- Your FitCoach trains you on the "10 Step" Program

- Your FitCoach will assess your current fitness level and individualize every aspect of your program to help you reach your goals.

- Learn how to perform the exercises properly to avoid injury while having productive and efficient workouts.

Find FitCoach information at www.FitCoaching.com or (866) 580-3229. Achieve the body you desire and deserve!

Joe Loiacano is the founder of FitCoaching.com and creator of the 10 Step Program for building the body of a champion. He has a reputation for transforming average people into well-defined body builders. He has been showcased on several body building magazine covers.
Contact him at Joe@FitCoaching.com.

No-Fail Solutions:
Food Strategies for Success
By Dr. Phil McGraw

For successful weight management, you must have in place particular plans for dealing with what you know will be the weakest spots in your efforts. Your particular weakness could be poor behavioral control, eating away from home, poor eating habits in general, splurging on vacations or during holidays, or overeating in response to stress. For example, do you typically drop in front of the TV with a bag of chips when you get home from work? In social situations, do you eat and drink far more than what is in keeping with your weight management goals? At restaurants, or on vacations, do you eat and drink far more than what is in keeping with your weight management goals? At restaurants, or on vacations, do you eat to your heart's content, without thinking about what this might do to your waistline?

Whatever your trouble spot is – and I'm sure you already know it – you need some strategies, skills, and solutions that will allow you to stop sabotaging yourself and your weight.

This chapter is designed to give you those skills, and help you consider ways in which you can begin to make each of them more of a daily element in your life. The more you try to apply these things, the more successful your weight management efforts will be. So start now. There are more than a hundred different ways you can change what is going on in your day-to-day life, and change your weight in the process. We will print only a few here for *Walking With the Wise for Health & Vitality*. A comprehensive list will be found in my *Ultimate Weight Solution Food Guide* which is available in most book stores.

Behavioral Strategies

You may get tired of hearing it, but I'll never get tired of repeating it. When you choose the behavior, you choose the consequences.

Much of your excess weight can be traced directly to specific behaviors that are driving your results. Before you get defensive and retreat into denial, make no mistake about the following. Whatever your weight, you set it up that way. This does not mean that you did it on purpose. Nevertheless, you are the responsible party. Until you reckon with this fact, you will have a difficult time getting your weight management efforts under control.

The good news is that you can choose differently from now on. You can behave your way to success. The following are positive steps you can take to help eliminate negative eating behaviors:

- Replace bad habits with incompatible actions. When you examine your own eating habits, and you get real about the fact that they are perpetuating your weight problem, then you need to eliminate them; you need to break those bad habits. "Break" is actually a misnomer, because we don't actually "break" habits. In order to eliminate one habitual behavior, you must replace it with a new behavior that is *incompatible* with the one you want to eliminate. When you make a new habit incompatible with the old one, the bad one will gradually lose its grip over you, since the two habits cannot coexist at the same time. For example, it is virtually impossible to spoon ice cream out of the carton if you are taking a shower. Taking a shower is incompatible with gorging on ice cream.

  One reason this plan of attack works so powerfully is that substituting an incompatible behavior for a bad habit takes your mind off the habit you want to weaken. When you are at work on activities such as gardening, playing with your kids, meditating, or journaling, your mind is usually not on food.

  So the trick is to enact one or more incompatible substitutes when you feel like overeating, or otherwise going off your food plan. These activities form a new cadre of coping tools that you can substitute for overeating. The more tools and activities you can plug into your day as coping strategies, the more likely you are to get the results you want.

- Change your eating style. Certain eating behaviors can lead to weight gain. These include eating too fast, snacking while watching television, sampling food while cooking, and eating in several rooms in your home, among other habits. These and other habits are examples of *mindless eating*, in which you shovel in an enormous amount of calories in a very short period of time without even realizing it. What you must do is replace mindless eating with its incompatible substitute, *mindful eating*, in which you concentrate on what and how you are eating. Mindful eating helps prevent overeating and leads to constructive behavioral change. What follows are some specific strategies you can use to counter mindless eating with mindful eating.

If you are a fast eater who needs to slow down:
- After your food is placed in front of you, wait five minutes before you eat it.
- Place small mouthfuls of food on your fork or in your spoon.
- Completely swallow food from each mouthful before you add any more to your fork or spoon.
- Put your utensils down between bites.
- Use smaller utensils (try a cocktail fork, for example) – no soup spoons, ladles, or otherwise oversize tableware for shoveling in food.
- Consciously take time to taste, chew, and savor the food you eat.
- Stretch out your meals, making them last thirty minutes instead of five or ten minutes, to allow for a reduction in hunger. One way to do this is to take a five-minute break at about ten minutes into your meal.
- Take sips of water or other noncaloric beverages between bites.
- Introduce a one- or two-minute delay between courses.

145

If you have trouble patrolling your portions:
- Measure your food if you're afraid of overeating.
- If you don't have the patience to measure out your food, use plates, glasses, and bowls in the serving sizes you need.
- Use a smaller plate for your meals.
- Purchase single-serving foods.
- Try the divided plate method of portion control. Fill half your plate with non-starchy vegetables, one fourth of your plate with a starchy carbohydrate, and the remaining fourth with a lean protein.

If you have a habit of eating leftovers:
- Put away all the food involved in preparing a meal.
- Have the table cleared of serving plates.
- Leave the table after you've finished eating.
- Have someone else clean leftovers off the plates after meals.
- Ask your family to scrape their plates directly into the garbage disposal after meals so that you won't be tempted to gorge on the leftovers.
- Leave some food on your plate.
- Purchase food in smaller packages or quantities so that you rarely have leftovers.

If you tend to eat while standing or while on the move:
- Localize your eating: Select one area of your home – your dining room, breakfast nook, or some other area reserved only for eating – and eat all of your food at a designated table in that area. That includes regular meals, snacks, and beverages.
- Vow to not eat while driving in your car; standing in front of your open refrigerator; reading a book, magazine, or newspaper; sitting in your bed; or talking on the phone. In other words, do not pair other behaviors with eating. Doing so only distracts your attention from your eating behavior, and you will lose all sense and awareness of how much you are consuming. If you are engaging in any of these behaviors while eating, you're not focused on your eating. This means you are not in control.
- Stop eating foods right out of their bags or packages.

If you sample food while cooking:
- Place a small portion of the food on a plate; sit down and taste it.
- Chew sugar-free gum while cooking.
- Minimize your time in the kitchen.
- Ask someone else in your family to occasionally prepare meals.

If your eating is chaotic and largely unplanned:
- Keep your personalized food diary. It is an effective tool for meal planning as well as a self-diagnostic tool for pinpointing small slips in your behavior before they become big ones. It lets you review and learn from your behaviors.
- Change your routine so that your drive to and from work doesn't take you by bakeries, fast-food restaurants, or other tempting eateries.
- Make food choices mindfully by asking yourself a simple question: "Does this food or meal, in the amount, contribute to my health and to effective weight control?" If the answer is no, if you are choosing to eat something,

or too much of something, that does not support your goal of health and weight management, then you need to rethink your decision.

If you overeat at night:
- Brush your teeth in the evening after dinner to signal that you've finished eating for the night.
- Read a book or magazine prior to going to bed; or substitute any activity you can think of that is incompatible with eating.

If you watch television while snacking:
- Eat only in your designated eating place – at your kitchen or dining room table.
- Eliminate all distractions while eating – including television (turn it off).
- Continue to keep problem foods out of your house, or else you'll indulge when an impulse to eat seizes you.

Mastering even one or two of the preceding bad behaviors will liberate you from counterproductive eating and dramatically reduce your weight. So if you want your weight to be lower than it has been in the past, get to work on these actions and disciplines. They will give you success.

Nutritional Strategies

Other areas for improvement may involve making some day-to-day tweaks in your nutrition and meal planning. Do you skip meals because you think you don't have enough time to eat? Do you go grocery shopping without a list and end up filling your pantry with foods you don't need? When you choose healthy foods, are you eating the same boring rabbit food, day after day, and now you're deep in a food rut that is causing you to rebel? You are about to find some extremely useful ways to help you create results that are better aligned with reaching your get-real weight. So let's put some more verbs in your sentences and some more action into your life with the following.

- Do not – I repeat, do not skip breakfast. Your body requires refueling after going eight to twelve hours without food. Not eating breakfast leads to cravings later and is a factor in overweight and obesity. If time is a problem in the morning: fix a breakfast shake or smoothie, made by blending fruit and low-fat milk; eat a bowl of packaged high-fiber cereal; or have a meal replacement bar or beverage, along with some fresh fruit.

- Expand your nutritional repertoire and try something new. Each week, introduce into your diet at least one fruit or vegetable you've never touched in the past.

- Cook "in bulk" on the weekends. Have cut-up vegetables ready for salads; mashed sweet potatoes ready for reheating; chili that can be microwaved; or chicken breasts that can be warmed up.

- Shop for "healthy" convenience foods, such as salad in a bag, so that you don't have to spend time chopping up salad vegetables.

- If you are in a hurry or too tired to cook and you must pop a packaged food into the microwave for a meal, at least serve it with a salad and fruit for dessert.

- Purchase more low-fat cooking gadgets – nonstick pots and pans, vegtable steamer, or rice cooker – to help you prepare more dishes that do not require the addition of fat.

- If you must help yourself to seconds, help yourself to vegetables.

- Cut the cocktails. Alcohol provides a triple whammy: It increases your appetite, lowers your inhibitions so you eat more, plus research shows that drinking alcohol will cause your body to store more calories as fat.

- Plan in advance when you will snack and what you will eat for that snack. This is far better – and safer – than unplanned snacking, for example, having a bag of chips or a bowl of candy that you mindlessly grab while watching TV or reading.

- Choose snacks from high-response cost, high-yield foods that supply good nutrition, rather than from nutritionally weak foods: a small bran muffin instead of a pastry, an apple instead of vending machine crackers, a glass of low-fat milk or soy milk instead of a soft drink.

- Take the same healthful snacks to work so that you won't be tempted by vending machine selections or fattening food brought in by your coworkers.

- Never eat any snack from its original container or package. Place it on a plate and eat your snack in a designated place.

- When grocery shopping:
  - Shop from a grocery list, prepared when you are not hungry or stressed out.
  - Determine exactly what you need for a particular period of time, and don't overbuy.
  - Stick to the outer aisles where the fresh, additive-free foods are located. There's a logical reason for this placement: Fresh foods require more frequent restocking and therefore must be situated as close to the out side shipping docks and stockrooms as possible.
  - Never go grocery shopping when you're hungry. The entire store, from the food aisles to the checkout line, can tempt you to buy foods that you neither want nor need.
  - Assign someone else in your family the job of grocery shopping on occasion in order to limit your exposure to food.

- Try not to use food as a reward when you've reached mile markers on the way to your get-real weight. This undoes any good you've done to yourself and shifts into reverse any progress you've made toward your weight loss goals. Instead, reward yourself with a new outfit, a new pair of walking shoes, a trip to a day spa, a new CD or DVD, or a special book.

What you have just read about are small, manageable changes you can easily make in activities you do every day. If you get practical about making these changes, you will begin the process of reprogramming yourself to get in the shape you want to be in.

Restaurant Strategies

For many of you, eating away from home, particularly at restaurants, is problematic. The key is to take some time to preplan for those situations and identify those things that could and should be the focus of your management efforts. When you decide to dine out:

- Select a restaurant that offers a variety of foods so that you can choose healthier menu items.

- Obtain a copy of the menu before going to a designated restaurant in order to decide ahead of time what you will order.

- Take control over the choice of restaurant. Go where you know you can order food that supports your weight control goals.

- Call the restaurant in question to determine whether they serve low-fat or low-calorie foods.

- Be assertive with the waitstaff; tell your server you want your food prepared without fats, oils, or sauces.

- Avoid all-you-can-eat and buffet-style restaurants or cafeterias, at least until you are less vulnerable to the sight of food. If you must go to a buffet-style restaurant, survey the entire buffet before you jump in line so that you can decide which selections are the healthiest and will support your weight control efforts. Use a smaller plate at buffet-style restaurants – either a salad plate or a dessert plate. Visit the food line only once; don't give in to the lure of the all-you-can-eat deal. Opt to order from the menu (if available), rather than choose from the buffet.

- Avoid ordering complete dinners, which often include unneeded portions, and opt instead for á la carte selections, since they give you more control over what you eat.

- If you know you are going to eat out for dinner, plan to have a lighter lunch to help balance and control calories.

- Say "no" to cocktails when dining out. Alcohol is high in sugar and calories, with the potential to contribute to weight gain. In addition, alcohol overstimulates your appetite and lowers your inhibitions about overeating.

- Ask the server to remove the bread basket after you've been served (hopefully your dinner companions will support you on this request). Removing the bread removes a huge temptation and source of extra calories.

- Curb your appetite by ordering a cup or bowl of broth-based soup, or a salad, prior to your meal.

- Stop sabotaging yourself with appetizers (other than a light soup or salad). The calorie counts of some of the most popular appetizers are through the roof. For example, fried onion rings = 2,000 calories; buffalo wings = 1,000 calories; cheese fries = 3,000 calories (eat those once a week and you can put on nearly a pound a week, or roughly 50 pounds a year!)

- Order high-response cost entrées– those that take time and effort to eat. Some suggestions: peel-and-eat steamed shrimp, steamed crab legs, artichokes, or a large dinner salad with dressing on the side.

- Get fluent in restaurant lingo. Sauces like béchamel, béarnaise, gratin, and hollandaise are synonyms for high fat and high cholesterol. *Sautéed* usually means cooked in butter. *Fried* is a red flag, since all fried food is loaded with fat and calories. So are gravy and cream sauces, since these are high in fat, cholesterol, and calories.

- Be clear, specific, and *polite* when making requests of your server. Simply state: "I'd like my chicken grilled dry, without butter, oil, or margarine."

- If you're feeling that your resolve is weak, have someone order for you. Make sure that someone is in your circle of support and will order a healthy, low-calorie entrée for you.

- When ordering a salad, ask for dressing on the side, order half the dressing, or request no dressing at all (opt for lemon or vinegar instead).

- Consider sharing an entrée with your dining companion, particularly if the restaurant is known for over-sizing or supersizing its portions.

- When ordering beef, stick to lower-fat cuts. These include London broil, sirloin, flank steak, and tender-loin. Lower-fat pork and veal selections include pork chops, pork loin, veal chops, and roast veal. (High-fat meats include prime rib, chopped steak made from chuck, ground lamb or pork, spareribs, and pork sausages.)

- Trim all visible fat from your meat.

- For poultry, order skinless chicken or turkey, while generally staying away from goose or duck (which tend to be higher in fat).

- Stick to entrées that are cooked by simple methods, such as broiling, baking, steaming, roasting, or braising. Fancier dishes such as casseroles are very likely to contain elevated levels of fat, calories, cholesterol, and sodium.

- Your best bets for breakfast at restaurants include hot and cold cereals (unsugared), fresh fruit, unsweetened fruit juices (small size), skim milk, artificially sweetened low-fat yogurt, or eggs, scrambled egg whites, or scrambled egg substitutes. Avoid large or jumbo muffins (they're loaded with fat, sugar, and calories); and pancakes, waffles, or French toast (which are usually prepared on a greased griddle).

- For lunch, avoid the urge to choose quick-to-eat low-response cost foods when time is at a premium (as it usually is during the lunch hour). Stick to salads with dressing on the side, while staying away from potato salad, macaroni salad, and coleslaw, which is usually made with a ton of mayonnaise. Sandwiches made with whole wheat bread or pita bread and white-meat poultry or lean roast beef are preferable to cheeseburgers or sandwiches prepared with high-fat lunch meats like salami, corned beef, or pastrami.

- Practice salad bar smarts. Stick to leafy greens and lettuces, fresh vegetables, and reduced-fat dressing. Don't spoon dressing over your salad; instead, pour it into a small bowl so that you can use a small, designated amount on your salad.

- Be aware of fattening additives lurking in certain salad bar items. Three-bean salad, for example, is high in sugar. Cottage cheese at some salad bars is of the whole-milk variety and therefore high in fat. So are pre-pared salads (again – potato salad, macaroni salad, and coleslaw), as well as shredded cheese. Bacon bits, pickles, and olives are high in sodium.

- A lot of restaurants will make up a vegetable plate for you if you ask them.

- Practice your behavioral eating-style skills not just at home, but also at restaurants: After your food is placed in front of you, wait five minutes before you eat it. Place small mouthfuls of food on your fork or in your spoon. Pause between bites and put your utensils down. Completely swallow food from each mouthful before you add any more to your fork or spoon. Consciously take time to taste, chew, and savor the food you eat. Take sips of water or other noncalorie beverages between bites.

- For dessert, choose fresh fruit, fruit salad, or sorbet (which is usually fat-free but higher in sugar).

- Don't feel guilty about leaving food on your plate. Do it!

- Ask the server to not bring the dessert cart to your table.

- Do an audit of your "dining out frequency." Count up how many times a week you eat out at restaurants. If your frequency is excessive – such as seven or more times – then you need to rethink your dining-out habits. People generally tend to eat more food when dining out. Plus, there is a lot of hidden fat and sugar in menu items you'd think were low-cal, so you may be sabotaging yourself unnecessarily here. Make a commitment to eat out no more than once or twice a week (such as on Friday evenings to celebrate the end of the workweek), or on special occasions such as a birthday or anniversary. Make eating out an event, not an everyday occurrence.

Travel and Vacation Strategies

Traveling and taking vacations can be difficult too, but try to exert the same control in your choice making that you would do at home or when eating out. If you're having difficulty in these areas, here are some strategies worth enacting;

- If you are flying, you don't have to settle for the typical airline food. If traveling by air, call the airline ahead of time (usually twenty-four hours) to request a special meal. Airlines can usually accommodate diabetic, vegetarian, low-fat, low-calorie, and low-sodium meals. You can make such requests practically anywhere, even on cruises, as long as you give the food preparation personnel plenty of notice.

- If the circumstances are such that you simply cannot control your choices, take it easy and eat smaller portions.

- If possible, take your own food to guarantee some control over what you eat while traveling or on vacation.

- Never travel on an empty stomach. This makes you less likely to cave in to food cues, such as fast-food vendors at airports. Eat a healthy, filling meal before you start your trip. If feasible, consider packing light and healthful snack foods, such as fresh or dried fruits, or cut-up vegetables.

- Self-monitor your food intake while away from home, using your personalized food diary and this food guide to help you stay the course. Pack both of these items.

- If your alcohol consumption tends to increase while on vacation, devise strategies to compensate, such as ordering club soda, diet drinks, or other nonalcoholic, but low-calorie beverages.

- Do not take a vacation from your workouts. Stay with your regular exercise program by walking, using hotel exercise facilities, or purchasing a week's membership at a local gym. During layovers, walk briskly around the airport for exercise. Exercising will burn off extra calories, plus help relieve the stress that is so often associated with traveling.

Social Strategies

Staying the course during special occasions such as holidays, parties, or celebrations can be a challenge unless you have plans in place to deal with the circumstances. Make a deal with yourself that you will try at least one or two of these the next time you are confronted with a social situation that makes it tempting to overeat or disregard your food plan:

- Plan ahead. On days when you'll be attending parties or get-togethers, consume fewer calories by eating a light breakfast and lunch. "Bank," or save, most of your calories for later on.

- Continue to self-monitor during the holidays by writing down what you eat and how many calories you consume in your personalized food diary. Research suggests that people who self-monitor their food intake can and will lose weight during the holidays.

- Consider a "Prediet." Try losing two or three pounds prior to the holidays to give yourself some room to move up the scales.

- Eat something light before you go to a party in order to avoid arriving too hungry. If you let yourself get too hungry, your stomach and your eyes will make your food choices for you, instead of your brain.

- Concentrate more on people and conversation at parties, and less on the food or drinks.

- Make the most nutritious choices possible at parties or gatherings: fresh fruits, raw vegetables, whole grain crackers, or lean proteins.

- If you are the host or hostess, there is no rule of hospitality that says you must serve fattening food for your guests. Try concocting lower-fat foods by altering recipes and using low-fat substitutes for high-fat ingredients. For example, you can replace all or part of the sour cream in dip recipes with plain low-fat yogurt. High-fat cheeses can be replaced by lower-fat products. You can also use reduced quantities of salt, sugar, and other sweeteners in recipes.

- Deal effectively with saboteurs. Your friends and family may present the biggest challenges to changes you want to make, especially at family get-togethers and celebrations. Sometimes friends and family won't take no for an answer and want to push food at you. In cases like this, try replies like, "No thanks, I just ate." "Can't have that. Doctor's orders." "Can you wrap it for me?" (Then toss it once you get home.) "Better not. An extra helping means an extra workout this week." "I'd love to, but I've got that class reunion coming up."

Guard against feeling guilty for focusing attention on yourself and standing up for yourself. It's okay to make time for yourself so that you

www.mentorsmagazine.com

can make your goals. You must take care of yourself before you can take care of others, and now is the time to do that.

- Take control of the social situation. If you're invited to an event where mostly low-response cost, low-yield foods will be served, graciously ask the host or hostess if you can bring some of your own food. Or be direct. Explain why you are not eating certain foods. You may be surprised at how some people may start supporting you when you stand up for yourself like this.

If, after all your planning and good intentions, you do overindulge, don't go on a guilt trip. Guilt is a useless emotion that only weakens your resolve to successfully manage your weight. Get over it and move on.

Stress-Eating Strategies

Never in your life will you be without stress – problems, challenges, and difficult moments that are simply a part of living. You know that if things are going well at work, for example, you can count on conflict at home, or vice versa. There is rarely a time in your life when all is at peace and balanced. That's not good or bad; it's simply the ebb and flow of how life works. To be alive means to experience stress.

With stressful situations comes the potential for overeating as a way to escape anxiety and pressure. If you're someone who struggles with your weight, then I'm willing to bet that you medicate with food as a stress reliever a good deal of the time, abusing food because it provides comfort and consolation when you are worried, irritated, annoyed, lonely, bored, or depressed.

Stress – particularly when it is prolonged and unresolved – provokes weight-sustaining physiological changes in your body. When you are under stress, your body releases stress hormones that automatically stimulate your appetite and set off cravings, prompting you to eat huge quantities of fattening food. These stress hormones trigger other bodily changes that may result in greater fat distribution around your waist. Overeating as a way to cope with stress may prove fatal to your weight-management efforts. You've got to step up and out of this behavior. Take a moment now to consider some of the following strategies:

- Be accountable for how you react to stress. One of my life laws states that *there is no reality; only perception.* What this means is that you are account able for how you respond to everything in your life. Whether it's an infu-riating phone call, a lost opportunity, or a person who has treated you poorly, your response to that event creates your experience.

- But behind that response is a perception – the way you interpret or assign meaning to what you are experiencing. If your response (your interpretation) to a stressor is typically negative, pessimistic, or gloom-and-doom, you are creating an experience for yourself that is self-defeating and infinitely more stress provoking. On the other hand, if you interpret the situation more positively, or realistically, you won't be so likely to become unglued, fall apart, or go into a panic mode.

When it comes to how you see things, you do have choices. You choose the reactions that create your level of stress. You have the power to choose your own perceptions and your own reactions; start choosing differently, with more clarity, more confidence, and more self-control. If you shake up your belief system and test your typical perceptions and reactions to events, rather than blindly or habitually holding on to them, the freshness of your new perspective can be startling. The freshness of your perspective can keep you from falling apart and resorting to food when the going gets tough. (Reading key 2, Healing Feelings, in *The Ultimate Weight Solution* will give you additional insights for managing the stress in your life and the emotions it produces.)

- Take a problem-solving approach to stress. Confront head-on whatever is wrong in your life and do something about it. If you don't, if you let these problems go unchallenged, you will pay the price and set yourself up for further physical and mental breakdown. The push to resolve the stress-provoking situation must come from you. You can either sit around and stew about the stressful situation or you can make the choice to be self-directed, take action, and adopt a solution-side approach to your life.

- Nourish your body with healthy alternatives. There are nutritious foods that will induce the same calming effect as high-sugar comfort foods, but without the unpleasant side effects. Among the most effective anxiety-management foods are fresh fruits, vegetables, and whole grains. Specifically, these foods are natural carbohydrates, which release serotonin, a brain chemical that lifts and improves your mood. Green leafy vegetables such as spinach and Romaine lettuce are bursting with a vitamin called folic acid, a mood-balancing nutrient. Other good-mood foods include fish and unprocessed turkey. Fish, in particular, is a food that has been linked to a lower incidence of depression because of the brain-healthy fats it contains.

The point is, for emotional comfort from food, you have to build certain foods into your food plan to help you normalize your mood for the day. This is nutritional knowledge that you can put to use on a day-to-day basis. Rather than sabotage your body's true needs, you can support them with high-nourishment foods.

- Practice relaxation. If you're stressed out and treat yourself to a plate of cookies or a bag of candy because you "deserve it," get real. There are other ways to treat yourself and restore calm without resorting to a food binge. That's why you must carve out time in your life for tension-reducing activities. I suspect that if you habitually overeat in reaction to stress, then you have no clue as to how to relax without a food binge. You are more accustomed to putting something fattening in your mouth to get relief rather than using nonfood activities to calm yourself down.

These alternatives include, but are not limited to exercising (a powerful stress reliever!), performing relaxation exercises, and listening to music. According to most research, these activities work directly on your nervous system by releasing endorphins, the brain's natural tranquilizers, to produce a state of reduced anxiety and a feeling of calm. These activities are natural, non-chemical, and inexpensive relaxants.

There's no good reason for you to experience any nutritional backsliding when you have strategies in place to handle it. When these situations arise, as you know they will, you won't panic and start eating everything in sight. You will simply say to yourself, "This is the very thing I knew would happen, and I know how to deal with it. I won't panic, and I won't give in just because I am encountering normal challenges of day-to-day life. I am in control."

As you manage your weight, never lose sight of the stakes involved. Your stakes are your health, your emotional well-being, your hopes and dreams, and the quality of your entire life. If you choose to bail out on managing your weight, be prepared to be another casualty of poor lifestyle decisions and choices.

Each day of progress you make, each action you take, has a positive effect. Trust in your ability to do it, and never forget that small and subtle changes in what you do are moving you in the right direction.

Phillip C. McGraw, Ph.D., is the #1 *New York Times* bestselling author of *Life Strategies, Relationship Rescue, Self Matters,* and the *Ultimate Weight Solution.* He is the host of the nationally syndicated, daily one-hour series *Dr. Phil,* One of the world's foremost experts in the field of human functioning, Dr. McGraw is the cofounder of Courtroom Sciences, Inc., the world's leading litigation consulting firm. Dr. McGraw currently lives in Los Angeles, California, with his wife and two sons. Visit his website: www.drphil.com

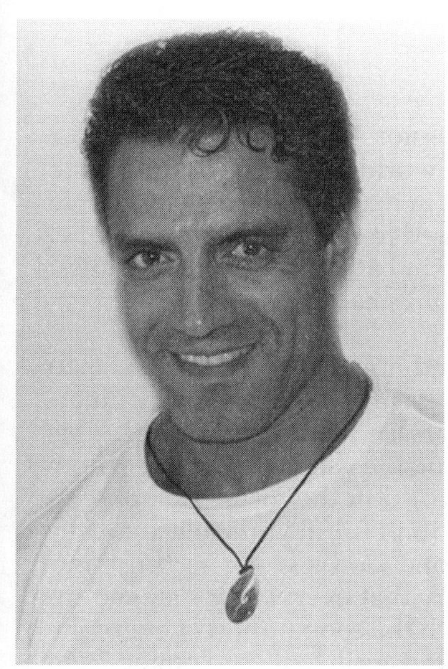

Mindful Fitness

vs

Fitness Obsession

By Nordine G. Zouareg

Mr. World / Mr. Universe
Fitness Manager at Miraval, Life In Balance

Mindfulness is being aware of your present moment. You are not judging, reflecting or thinking. You are simply observing the moment in which you find yourself. Moments are like a breath. The next breath replaces each breath. You're there with no other purpose than being awake and aware of that moment. As my yogi master, Yogi Bhajan said: "If you don't go within, you go without!"

Why not practice the same approach to physical fitness? Use each repetition, each set of every exercise to its fullest potential as if it was the last time you were performing the exercise.

If you start by being aware of your breath and connect it to each repetition - breathe in when you come down, breathe out when you come up - you know it comes and goes. It is like the end of one wave from among the endless ocean waves. They continue to come and disappear, to be followed by another and another and another. They come. They disappear. They come, they end, and they flow back to be covered by another incoming wave. You can hear the sound. Its rhythm puts the mind and the heart into a trance, and you go far away...but wherever you go, there you are.

My travels through this journey called life have taken me down many paths from which I now share some reflections on the *"Holistic approach of fitness."* The feeling good, looking good approach, rather than the looking good and then what? This is what I call the *"connected"* kind of attitude.

We are infatuated with fitness. We pay attention to our waistlines. We get liposuction. We get breast implants. We buy special cosmetic products. We try our best to look and feel our best. We tighten our skin, harden our bodies, increase our cardiovascular endurance and increase our lung capacities. We try to keep ourselves fit. But what about our spiritual fitness? There is no supplement for spirituality. There is no reduced calorie spirituality. There is no "Quick Fix" for seeking the goodness that is within us. The path is taken when you are on it.

My personal experience with the fitness obsession started the minute I lost control of my inner self. I wanted to please the world. I thought people were expecting me to be at a top level all the time, but in reality it was not so. People loved me then like they love now. They don't need to see me in a super shape. I just have to be me, love me and love them. Be in balance - that's all it takes. Love is the door to your spiritual, mental and physical fitness.

In other articles I will tell my many stories and how I went from Rickets to a Mr. Universe lifestyle, and from obsession to the manifestation of my inner-self over my outer self. *The Holistic Fitness approach* sees you as a gift. This doesn't change, regardless of whether you get outside validation or not. Know and remember that you are God's gift to the world in the form you are. You are an indispensable part of God's plan. If you don't fulfill your role joyously, even if it is unpopular, you will not have done God's work as fully and completely as you could. Assume the possibility that everybody's signed up in advance for the roles they play right now, with the cooperation of everyone being affected by those roles. Self-judgment and guilt will no longer have anyplace to stick. The dance that we do is one that encourages us to remember and directly connect with the source of all life here in this world.

Imagine feeling better than you ever have. Imagine looking better than you ever have.

Imagine the physical vitality spilling over into every aspect of your life. If all of your workouts, diets, and efforts have not gotten you to the fitness level you want to be at, there may be a missing connection. A connection of self, a connection into the *spirit.*

Nordine has won body building/fitness championships throughout the world by relying on training strategies he developed based on his extensive educational background and his 23 years experience in the fitness field. Nordine went on to claim the titles of Mr. France, Mr. Europe, Mr. International, Mr. World and ultimately Mr. Universe. Now Nordine is offering his expertise in one of the most prestigious Health Spa Resorts: Miraval, Life in Balance. The "Miraval experience" is a diverse and exhilarating range of activities, pampering guest services, and innovative cuisine along with an internationally recognized spa, allowing one to experience the ultimate in a resort destination. It's a place where one can connect with life, health, meaning and purpose. More than a vacation, it is a place where you can appreciate the moment and bring life into balance. If you would like to work out with Nordine, you can find him at Miraval, Life in Balance Spa and Resort in Tucson, Arizona. Website: www.miravalresort.com or call 1-800-232-3969. Mention this book when making your reservation and you will receive a special rate. You can also contact Nordine at www.totalbodywork.com.

The Seven Cornerstones of a Strong Body and Strong Mind

By Shawn Phillips

I was recently being interviewed for an article and doing what I often do: answering questions about exercise, nutrition and getting in shape. The questions are generally the same, and so are the answers (the truth never changes). However, about an hour in I was asked a question I have *not* answered 100 times. In fact, it was a question I hadn't really given much thought prior to the moment the reporter asked, "Shawn, in these troubled times – in this uncertain, downright frightening post-9/11 world, why even bother trying to get in shape, much less build a strong, lean body?"

Typically I answer questions quickly, but this time, the answer didn't come right away. I took a deep breath, leaned back in my chair and gazed out the window. A few minutes in contemplation and I saw the 'bigger picture' – the importance of fitness was clear, like I've never quite seen it before. So I leaned forward and, with clarity and confidence, shared how I see it...

First of all, taking care of yourself and doing what you can to become as healthy and fit as possible matters now more than ever. I believe a strong nation is made up of strong people. And one thing every person in this country can do to help strengthen America is strengthen themselves.

Next, there's the economical impact on our country. Each year, U.S. taxpayers spend over $100 billion caring for Americans who didn't take care of themselves. That money goes to treat people who are suffering from obesity (an alarming 67% of Americans) and its secondary diseases such as diabetes, heart disease, vascular disease, cancer and other debilitating diseases. So if you just look at it from a fiscal standpoint, you can see how vitally important it is to make sure we don't become a burden to our country.

Then there's the mental aspect. When you strengthen the body, you strengthen the mind. You strengthen individual character and courage.

www.mentorsmagazine.com

Today, more than ever, people need a healthy way to deal with the uncertainty, anxiety, stress and confusion. Now consider the fact that it has been scientifically proven that regular, intense exercise, along with healthy eating, elevates energy levels, keeps the mind clear, reduces depression and stress. That, in turn, improves quality of life.

Now, I'm not saying we should become obsessed with fitness or building a muscular body. I am saying it's a worthwhile goal. When you look fit, lean and strong, you're also going to be healthy on the inside.

Over the last decade I've helped thousands of fitness buffs, athletes and celebrities build strong, lean, healthy bodies. And what I've discovered is that regardless of whether you want to trim down, build up or firm all over, it is very important to understand and accept that there is no 'one thing,' no magic potion, single exercise or diet that will allow you to sculpt a healthy, toned physique.

The simple truth is that the 'one thing' many people seek is 'everything!' How you feed your body, the way you think and even how you stay motivated has every bit as much to do with how you look as the exercises you do. The following 'Seven Cornerstones to a Strong Body and Strong Mind' are the 'everything': the fundamentals I've seen that produce remarkable results time and time again.

1. Train With Weights

I've no doubt that you're aware of how vital exercise is to your health. Unfortunately, far too many people who do exercise only exercise one muscle – the heart. I agree that maintaining a healthy heart is serious business. But if you're not paying the same attention to the other (700) muscles in your body, you're missing out on some of the most potent benefits of exercise.

The single most powerful way to build strong, defined muscles and burn more fat for a lean body is by training your entire body with weights regularly – with intensity. And as weight training helps build strong muscle and maintain strength and flexibility, it is even more vital as one ages.

2. Supercharge Fat Loss

You may hear a lot about 'metabolism' these days. All you really need to know is that the 'faster' your metabolism, the more energy (and fat) your body uses to sustain normal living. Contrary to what many people believe, there are simple things you can do to speed up your metabolism and create a more energized, healthier state and a leaner body.

To boost your metabolism, start eating smaller, more frequent meals throughout the day, increase the amount of protein in your diet, do high-intensity cardiovascular workouts and, of course, resistance train to increase your muscle mass. All of those factors combined can be powerful fat burner on their own.

3. Get Clear

It has been estimated that 98% of people who commit to getting in shape each New Year fail to follow through. One reason is that they never set a specific goal. A goal of 'getting in shape' is like a financial goal of earning 'lots of money.' Neither is more than a dream – not until you've made the goal explicit and put pencil to paper to record it.

Don't make the mistake of setting 'fitness dreams.' Yes, your goals should be lofty and the thought of achieving them should give you energy deep inside, but you should also be able to convince a jury you believe you can achieve it.

For the next 12 weeks, decide exactly how much muscle you want to gain and exactly how much fat you want to lose! 'A few pounds' will not do.

4. Have A Plan

I'll bet you learned early on, like I did, that there are 'no shortcuts' in life. Darn good advice, but unfortunately, many people have taken this to mean they must always find the hardest possible way to success. Please don't make this any more challenging than it already is. I learned long ago the wisdom of following in the footsteps of those who have succeeded before me. My advice to you is to take this 'shortcut' and find someone who's achieved the results you would like to realize and do what he or she did. If you follow a proven plan, you may very well achieve spectacular results as well!

5. Measure Progress

Sustaining the motivation toward achieving your goal is without question one of the greatest challenges in all of fitness. It requires unwavering determination, discipline and faith, and regular, consistent feedback on your progress. A simple method of measuring results will provide that all-important feedback: trust me, when you see real progress, it fuels a fire like nothing else.

Given that muscle weighs considerably more than fat, relying on the scale alone is a mistake. A simple cloth tape measure can be a perfect complement to a bathroom scale. Each morning I step on the scale, weigh myself and use the tape to measure my waist (where I collect most of my bodyfat). I then record this in my 'Success Journal.' I watch the weekly trends and adjust my plan accordingly until I am getting the results I want!

6. Aim High

In the last decade, I've met thousands of people who need to 'drop about 5 pounds.' See the same people six months later, and, you got it, they still need to drop 'five pounds.' Why don't they get on with it? Simple, it's not a significant enough goal. Most people reach only as far as they know their arm will extend, setting goals that lack the 'magic' to access the energy deep in their souls. Don't make this mistake. Instead, set your sights high, outside your reach. Allow yourself to imagine your body looking and feeling a way that ignites a burning desire inside. Shoot for the stars and enjoy the ride.

7. Get Focused!

If you find exercise 'boring' or it's just not 'stimulating enough,' get 'focused.' Focus means you put everything you have into what you're doing at that very second – whether it's your work, workout or nutrition, or a friend, family member or loved one. Absolutely nothing else matters during that given moment.

The ability to focus the energy of your mind and body like the light of an ordinary fluorescent bulb to the concentrated intensity of a laser beam is a powerfully important concept and an absolute breakthrough strategy – for exercise and for life. And, in my mind, there's no better place to develop your ability to focus than during physical exercise – to train your mind along with your body.

Final Thoughts

I've discovered that people who succeed in dramatically transforming their physiques – those who build a strong, healthy body – become so empowered that they can change many other things in their lives. By building a better body, you'll have greater self-esteem, more confidence and a better attitude. So if you want to improve in any areas of your life, start by focusing on building a better body, and let that flow into other areas of your life.

Shawn Phillips is an innovator, speaker, expert coach and the author
of *ABSolution, The Practical Solution for Building Your Best Abs*. For over a
decade, Shawn's helped athletes, celebrities and fitness buffs build strong,
healthy bodies with his commonsense approach to fitness. To receive
Shawn's insightful tips for building your best abs and body,
visit *www.BestABS.com*.

Life is a
Balancing Act

By Mark Victor Hansen

Life on a Tightrope

Imagine a tightrope walker in circus. He is on a rope suspended a few feet above the straw covered floor. His purpose is to walk the rope from one end to other. He holds a long bar in his hands to help him maintain his balance. But he must do more than simply walk. On his shoulders he balances a chair. And in that chair sits a young woman who is herself balancing a rod on her forehead, and on top of that rod is a plate.

If at any time one of the items should start to drift off balance, he must stop until he can get all of them in perfect alignment again. The tightrope artist doesn't begin until all the elements above him are aligned. Only then does he move forward, carefully, slowly across the rope.

I suggest that life is very much a balancing act and that we are always just a step away from a fall. We are constantly trying to move forward with our purpose, to achieve our goals, all the while trying to keep in balance the various elements of our lives.

Getting Out of Balance

Many of us get out of balance with regard to money. If we don't have sufficient money, then our lives become a money chase. We constantly devote our energies toward improving our finances. In the process we tend to take energy away from our family, our mate, our spiritual and mental needs, even our health. More importantly, we don't move forward toward our life purpose. We don't proceed along the tightrope. Only when we get our finances straightened out can we spread our energies to all the other aspects of our life and proceed with our purpose.

Other areas of our life could be out of harmony. It could be our relationship with our wife or husband. It could be a spiritual emptiness that is gnawing at our insides. It could be lack of appropriate social contact. It could be illness. If any aspect of our life draws a disproportionate amount of energy, we have to shortchange the other aspects. This throws us off and we are unable to move forward on life's tightrope until a balance can be reestablished.

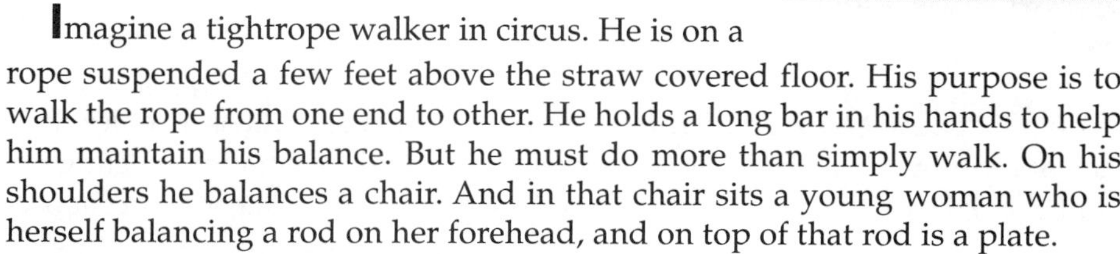

www.mentorsmagazine.com

Getting in Balance

Our first priority, therefore, is getting our life in balance. We need to deal with any areas that are taking too much energy and put them in perspective – align them so that we have energy available for all areas.

We need to create a balance of winning identities as father or mother, lover, husband, or wife, son or daughter, worker, participant, finisher and so forth. Only when each identity is fulfilled will that area be functioning and not overdrawing our energy.

But this doesn't happen by itself. Achieving a balanced life is a choice that each of is continually makes second by second, thought by thought, feeling by feeling. On the one hand, we can simply exist. But on the other, we can choose to pack out seconds and create valuable minutes in all aspects of our lives.

It's important to understand that others cannot do this for us. I can be me, and only you can be you. No one can think, breathe, feel, see, experience, love or die for either of us. Inside, we are what we are. We all come into life without a map, an operating manual or a definition of ourselves, other than male or female. It's up to us to balance all the different aspects of our lives. We can do to by pushing the 'decide' buttons in our lives.

Making an Assessment

At first it's important to stop and assess how we're doing. We should look at all the various aspects of our life that we are constantly juggling, constantly trying to keep in balance. These include: marriage and family, finances, health, social contact, spiritual development and mental growth.

Are we able to devote ample energy to all areas? Or are we tipped off to one side, unbalanced in one direction?

Steps to Achieving Balance In Your Life

1. **Assess your life as it is now.** Looking at ourselves as we really are is the first step in re-creating our lives. Do you feel physically exhausted, mentally stagnant, or find yourself without close relationships? Would you call yourself a workaholic? Do you feel a lack of spiritual alignment? If you answer yes to any of these questions, your life is probably out of balance.

2. **Make a conscious decision to become balanced.** Choosing reality as our basis of decision is the second step to becoming balanced. Achieving balance allows us to reach our goals and our purpose in life while creating less stress to do so. A conscious decision to change is now in order.

3. **Re-make that decision on a minute-to-minute basis.** We are all instant forgetters. Remember all those New Year resolutions? Renewing our decisions on a daily, minute to minute basis allows us to ease into change, instead of expecting things to change overnight.

4. **Set goals in every area of your life.** Set realistic goals in all areas of your life to assist yourself in remembering that your ultimate goal is balance. Your goal should cover:

   - Relationships, both at home and in the marketplace.
   - Physical beingness.
   - Spiritual alignment.
   - Mental development.
   - Your job.
   - Finances.

5. **Be willing to take the risk.** Being willing to assess yourself and take the risk to change will not only enhance your life, but you will feel more energy and an expanded awareness of what life is all about. Acknowledging that balance is essential, and recreating your life to encompass your decision is worth all the risk.

6. **Make time to re-assess yourself on a daily basis.** None of us can really know how well we are doing with change in our lives unless we are willing to re-assess our position. Don't feel that your decisions are made in concrete. If something feels that it isn't working, be willing to look at a new decision. Make time for yourself every day, in a quiet meditative state, to relax and 'check yourself out.'

© 2002 Mark Victor Hansen

Mark Victor Hansen is the co-author of the wildly successful *Chicken Soup for the Soul* series and his newest book, *The One Minute Millionaire.* He is also founder of the fast-growing internet-based *Goal-Mining Challenge*, a free resource for people to learn how to set goals in every facet of life for immediate, and amazing, improvement. To learn more, visit *www.markvictorhansen.com.*

Learning Not to Age:
The Link Between Belief and Biology

By Deepak Chopra, M.D.

Although awareness gets programmed in thousands of ways, the most convincing are what we call beliefs. A belief is something you hold on to because you think it is true. But unlike a thought, which actively forms words or images in your brain, a belief is generally silent. A person suffering from claustrophobia doesn't need to think, "This room is too small," or, "There are too many people in this crowd." Put into a small, crowded room, his body reacts automatically. Somewhere in his awareness is a hidden belief that generates all the physical symptoms of fear without his having to think about it. The flow of adrenaline that causes his pounding heart, sweaty palms, panting breath, and dizziness is triggered at a level deeper than the thinking mind.

People with phobias struggle desperately to use thoughts to thwart their fear, but to no avail. The habit of fear has sunk so deep that the body remembers to carry it out, even when the mind is resisting with all its might. The thoughts of a claustrophobic – "There's no reason to be afraid," "Small rooms aren't dangerous," "Everyone else looks perfectly normal, why can't I get over this?" – are rational objections, but the body acts on commands that override thought.

Our beliefs in aging hold just this kind of power over us. Let me give an example. For the past twenty years, gerontologists have performed experiments to prove that remaining active throughout life, even up to one's late seventies, would halt the loss of muscle and skeletal tissue. The news spread among retired people that they should continue to walk, jog, swim, and keep up their housework; under the slogan "Use it or lose it," millions of people now expect to remain strong in old age. With this new belief in place, something once considered impossible happened.

Daring gerontologists at Tufts University visited a nursing home, selected a group of the frailest residents, and put them on a weight-training regimen. One might fear that a sudden introduction to exercise would exhaust or kill these fragile people, but in fact they thrived. Within eight weeks, wasted muscles had come back by 300 percent, coordination and balance improved, and overall a sense of active life returned. Some of the subjects who had not been able to walk unaided could now get up and go to the bathroom in the middle of the night by themselves, an act of reclaimed dignity that is by no means trivial. What makes this accomplishment truly wondrous, however, is that the youngest subject in the group was 87 and the oldest 96.

These results were always possible; nothing new was added here to the capacity of the human body. All that happened was that a belief changed, and when that happened, aging changed. If you are 96 years old and afraid to move your body, it will waste away. To go into a weight-training room at that age, you have to believe that it will do your body good, you have to be free of fear, and you have to believe in yourself. When I say that aging is the result of a belief, I'm not implying that a person can simply think aging away. Exactly the opposite – the stronger the belief, the more rooted in the body it is and the more immune to conscious control.

According to the belief system you and I adhere to, Nature has trapped us in bodies that grow old against our will. The tradition of aging extends as far back as recorded history and even prehistory. Animals and plants grow old, fulfilling a universal law of Nature. It is hard to imagine that aging is the result of learned behavior, for biology cannot be denied.

Yet the core belief that aging is a fixed, mechanical process – something that just happens to us – is only a belief. As such, it blinds us to all kinds of facts that don't fit the belief system we cling to. How many of the following statements do you believe are facts?

a) Aging is natural – all organisms grow old and die.

b) Aging is inevitable – it can't be prevented.

c) Aging is normal – it affects everyone about the same.

d) Aging is genetic – I'll probably live about as long as my parents and grandparents did.

e) Aging is painful – it causes physical and mental suffering.

f) Aging is universal – the law of entropy makes all orderly systems run down and decay.

g) Aging is fatal – we're all growing old and dying.

If you take any or all of these to be statements of fact, you are under the influence of beliefs that do not match reality. Each statement contains a little objective truth, but each can be refuted, too.

a) Aging is natural, but there are organisms that never age, such as one-celled amoebas, algae, and protozoa. Parts of you also do not age – your emotions, ego, personality type, IQ, and other mental characteristics, for example, as well as vast portions of your DNA. Physically, it makes no sense to say that the water and minerals in your body are aging, for what is "old water" or "old salt?" These components alone make up 70 percent of your body.

b) Aging is inevitable, but the honeybee at certain times of the year can shift its hormones and completely reverse its age. In the human body, shifts in hormones may not be as dramatic, but there is enough latitude so that on any given day your hormonal profile may be younger than the day, month, or year before.

c) Aging is normal; however, there is no normal curve of aging that applies to everyone. Some people entirely escape certain aging symptoms, while others are afflicted with them long before old age sets in.

d) Aging has a genetic component that affects everyone, but not to the degree usually supposed. Having two parents who survived into their eighties adds only about three years to a child's life expectancy; less than 5 percent of the population has such good or bad genes that their life span will turn out to be significantly longer or shorter. By comparison, by adopting a healthy lifestyle, you can delay symptoms of aging by as much as thirty years.

e) Aging is often painful, both physically and mentally, but this is the result not of aging itself but of the many diseases that afflict the elderly; much of that disease can be prevented.

f) Aging seems to be universal, because all orderly systems break down over time, but our bodies resist this decay extremely well. Without negative influences from within and without, our tissues and organs could easily last 115 to 130 years before sheer age caused them to stop functioning.

g) Finally, aging is fatal, because everyone has to die, but in the vast majority of cases, perhaps as much as 99 percent, the cause of death is not old age but cancer, heart attack, stroke, pneumonia, and other illnesses.

It is extremely difficult to ascertain what it would be like to watch the body age per se. Two cars left out in the rain will rust at about the same rate; the process of oxidation attacks them equally, turning their iron and steel into ferrous oxide according to one easily explained law of chemistry. The aging process obeys no such simple laws. For some of us, aging is steady, uniform, and slow, like a tortoise crawling toward its destination. For others, aging is like approaching an unseen cliff – there is a long, secure plateau of health, followed by a sharp decline in the last year or two of life. And for still others, most of the body will remain healthy except for a weak link, such as the heart, which fails much faster than do the other organs. You would have to follow a person for most of his adult life before you figured out how he was aging, and by then it would be too late.

The fact that aging is so personal has proved very frustrating for medicine, which finds it extremely difficult to predict and treat many of the major conditions associated with old age. Two young women can ingest the same amount of calcium, display equally healthy hormone levels, and yet one will develop crippling osteoporosis after menopause while the other won't. Twin brothers with identical genes will go through life with remarkably similar medical histories, yet only one will develop Alzheimer's or arthritis or cancer. Two of the most common conditions in old age, rising blood pressure and elevated cholesterol, are just as unpredictable. The aging body refuses to behave according to mechanical laws and rules.

After decades of intense investigation, there is no adequate theory of human aging. Even our attempts to explain how animals age have resulted in more than three hundred separate theories, many of them contradictory. Our notions of aging have been drastically modified over the last two decades. In the early 1970s, doctors began to notice patients in their sixties and seventies whose bodies still functioned with the rigor and health of middle age. These people ate sensibly and looked after their bodies. Most did not smoke, having given up the habit sometime after the Surgeon General's original warnings about lung cancer in the early 1960s. They had never suffered heart attacks. Although they exhibited some of the accepted signs of old age – higher blood pressure and cholesterol, and tendencies to put on body fat, to become farsighted, and to lose the top range of their hearing – there was nothing elderly about these people. The "new old age," as it came to be called, was born.

The "old old age" had been marked by irreversible declines on all fronts – physical, mental, and social. For untold centuries people expected to reach old age – if they reached it at all – feeble, senile, socially useless, sick, and poor. To reinforce this grim expectation there were grim facts: Only one out of ten people lived to the age of 65 before this century.

For centuries in the past, the human body was exposed to the killing influence of a harsh environment: inadequate nutrition, a lifetime spent in physical labor, and uncontrollable epidemics of disease created conditions that accelerated aging. Leaf through the accounts of immigrants passing through Ellis Island at the turn of the century; some of the photographs will horrify you. The faces of 40-year-old women look haggard and drawn, literally as if they were 70 – and an old 70 at that. Adolescent boys look like battered middle-aged men. Under the surgeon's scalpel their hearts, lungs, kidneys, and livers would have looked identical to those of a modern person twice their age. Aging is the body's response to conditions imposed upon it, both inner and outer. The sands of age shift under our feet, adapting to how we live and who we are.

The new old age arrived on the scene after more than half a century of improved living conditions and intensive medical progress. The average American life span of 49 years in 1900 jumped to 75 in 1990. To put this huge increase in perspective, the years of life we have gained in less than a century are equal to the total life span that individuals enjoyed for more than four thousand years; from prehistoric times to the dawn of the Industrial Revolution, the average life span remained below 45. Only 10 percent of the general population used to make it to 65, but today 80 percent of the population lives at least that long.

At any one time, your health is the sum total of all the impulses, positive and negative, emanating from your consciousness. You are what you think. If you are happy, this just means that you have happy thoughts most of the time. If you are depressed, it means that you have sad thoughts most of the time. Into this calculation enter all our other states of mind as well: our daily share of anger, fear, envy, greed, kindness, compassion, benevolence, and love. These are all simply thoughts. When one of them happens to predominate, it leads to a corresponding state of mind and, as we have seen, to a corresponding state of physiology.

In fact, we can restate the evidence for the psychophysiological connection in one sentence: For every state of consciousness, there is a corresponding state of physiology. If you are having hostile thoughts, for example, they will be reflected in your mood, your facial expression, your social behavior, and how you feel physically. You scowl, you are impatient and difficult to deal with, you churn up too much acid in your stomach and a lot of adrenaline in your bloodstream, and consequently you may develop peptic ulcers and hypertension. For an observant person, it is not at all difficult literally to read your thoughts. And the cells of your body are registering them far more accurately.

In most people, the psychophysiological connection operates more or less randomly. Thoughts arise from interactions with the world, these thoughts affect the body for better or worse, and they leave a lingering impression in the form of moods, tendencies toward disease, actual disease symptoms, and the process of wearing out the body over time, which we call aging. Very little of this is under our conscious control. However, it is obvious that some thoughts are under our control, and this simple fact leaves an opening for further growth in the proper direction, toward mastery of the self.

Mastery of the self has classically been called "enlightenment." Enlightenment simply means having control over the psychophysiological connection. The highly evolved mind is not a prey to random influences of ill health; it has mastery over what it thinks. Therefore, what it thinks is happy and healthy. Mastery of this kind is not something peculiar or "not normal." It is simply an extension of the normal ability to control some thoughts. This natural capacity, when given room to expand and evolve, goes in one direction, and that is toward more perfect health and greater happiness. That is what Dr. Salk meant by survival of the wisest.

Because it is in the nature of life to evolve, we do not have to do anything to evolve in the proper direction. Gaining mastery of the self, with all its benefits to health, means little more than stepping out of the way and allowing the infinite intelligence of the mind and body to cooperate more fully. That is what they want to do. When we stop interfering and are wise enough to let the psychophysiological connection work for us instead of against us, our minds rush as quickly as possible towards perfect health.

For information on programs offered by Deepak Chopra, M.D.,
and mind/body health services, please contact:
the Chopra Center for Well Being
7630 Fay Avenue, La Jolla, CA 92037
(888) 424-6772 (toll-free) /(619) 551-7788
(619) 551-7811 (fax)
e-mail: info@chopra.com
website: www.chopra.com

The
Last Words
from
Usually Silent Observers...

© 2004 Kim Muslusky

The Domino Effect

By Lena Osborn

"It is time to celebrate your inherent greatness and to understand we were created perfectly. The body is a marvel that functions like no machine ever created by humans. Too many people treat their bodies (their only vehicle in life) as if they could get another when the first one is used up." — John Assaraf

When we walk with the wise and listen to their wisdom..WE become wise. When we apply the wisdom learned from the wise...OUR LIVES TRANSFORM.

How can we learn to be wise about our health? We can start by reading this book.

Once we start living a lifestyle that encourages vitality...a whole new world will open up to us. Life FEELS GOOD!!! It will also touch everything around you. The domino effect of changed action in your life has far reaching effects. For instance, a few examples would be in the areas of our children, families, business and everyday life.

Did you know that you are being watched by your children? Everything that you do on a daily basis will become ingrained in the memory of your child. This memory will teach them how to think and act in a particular way. They will then apply this learned behavior to their own lives as adults. Children learn more from your actions...from YOU, the person they love and want to be like. From there, children grow...have children of their own and then teach them what they know...generation after generation. (Unless a conscious effort is made to change a belief and/or lifestyle habits.) Remember back to your childhood. What do you remember about your parents? Are you living a wise lifestyle NOW? Do you want your lifestyle actions repeated generation after generation?

The lives of everyone in our families are affected by health. How would your demise or chronic illness affect those around you? How about your good health and vitality...what possibilities do you envision could evolve?

Then we have our business lives. The same question applies...bad health will create what domino effect? Good health and vitality will create what domino effect? Will it mean prosperity or poverty?

I could go on about multiple possibilities but I think you get the idea.

"YOUR HEALTH WILL AFFECT NOT ONLY YOUR LIFE...
BUT EVERYTHING AND EVERYBODY AROUND YOU
FOR A VERY LONG TIME."

You've taken an important first step by choosing to learn more. May the domino effect of your decision empower you and the ones you love in glorious and wonderful ways!!!

Lena Osborn is the Chief of Operations for Mentors International, Inc. She is in partnership with Linda Forsythe and is responsible for the International Division for Mentoring. Her career has spanned many countries in different continents – Europe, Asia, North and South America. She is an expert in many diverse fields, including law, television and film production, computer engineering, publishing and was also a model in France.
You may contact Lena at Lena@mentorsmagazine.com

Dear Reader

By Kim Muslusky

OK, so I'm thinking to myself yet again; what has SHE gotten me into this time!? (The "SHE" in question being our tenacious wonder woman / publisher, Linda Forsythe...) In my three-year odyssey with MENTORS Publications, I have walked down some pretty outrageous paths with this whirling dervish in search of inner growth and abundance. She continually manages to shake up my mundane reality while pushing me out of my too-comfortable, 20-pounds-too-heavy box...and the three-month time span spent working on this health book has been no exception.

I remember thinking at its inception, what could we possibly say in this tome that hasn't been done or said too many times before? What's left to make people get up off that comfy couch, put down those salty-too-many-calories-chips and beer, start moving their over weight tushes – and get responsible for their own health and well-being...?

I know. I have first-hand, real and personal experience at with the afore-mentioned decadence. For several years, I have been able to delude myself into thinking that I am physically fit. After all, I do own a gym membership – and I even go once or twice a week – most weeks. But, as the Art Director for this book, I have had to, of course, read all the articles included in it. Having done so, I now realize that there have been some major delusions keeping my addled, middle-aged brain hostage for quite some time. I need to make considerable alterations to become really healthy – to not continue to be just a once-a-week gym wannabe.

I'm 20 pounds overweight, I don't always eat nutritious food, and I like my glass of wine in the evening. I don't take vitamins, or minerals, I work far too many hours, and am over-stressed on too many occasions. Breakfast and lunch are eaten, if at all, in front of the computer screen. I have a bad back and I don't get enough sleep. And I'm just plain grumpy! And I don't do vacations, either. They tend to give me anxiety attacks about the work that I've left behind. Yada, yada, yada... whine, whine, whine...

The good news is that I do get to the dentist regularly, and I do love my poor dear husband...

This book presented me with a plethora of new concepts to address how I got to this point, and better yet: what I can do to make REAL positive changes. I really do want to dance at my grandkids' weddings - all six of them! All the *Walking with the Wise for Health and Vitality* contributors have provided valuable, practical information to improve my vigor and extend my life span. They have actually inspired me to make changes to my misbegotten habits. (Although, I think I still want to remain a grump...) I am eating more fresh fruit and vegetables, taking vitamins, and walking every day. I am using (I really am...) that gym membership, as well as trying to lighten-up in general...

As in past MENTORS projects, I hope my small part in this book will help make a difference in your life's journey and health, so that you too can dance at your grandchildrens' weddings!

Kim Muslusky is a designer/illustrator with over 27 years experience in the fine art, publishing, advertising, and TV/Video/Film industries.
You may contact her at 858-693-7380 or
kim@mentorsmagazine.com

 www.mentorsmagazine.com

Start Where You Are

By Cheri Hoffman

As the editor for *Walking With the Wise for Health and Vitality*, I have read every word of this book – several times. The thought that crossed my mind most often while reading all those words was, "Great. Now I'm responsible for this information. There goes the fabled bliss of ignorance."

Not that I could have honestly claimed ignorance. Who can, in our fitness-crazed yet more-overweight-than-ever-before society? The problem is less about a lack of knowledge and more about the lack of discipline to put that knowledge to use. I know that putting what I've learned into practice can only be for my good. It's just that it's hard. The sheer volume of incredibly wise advice from the experts in this book is overwhelming. There are so many things that we should do, and so many things we do that we shouldn't.

Don't despair. Whether your struggle is with weight, disease, attitude, or all of the above, there's something you can do. These pages are filled with practical steps toward health. You don't have to take them all at once. The important thing is that you take one.

I'm not a doctor or a nutritionist or a fitness expert. I can't tell you anything new about getting or staying healthy. The best advice I can offer is to start on the journey toward health *now*. No matter where you are, start from there. Yesterday's choices were yesterday's, and there's nothing to be done about them now except to make better – and healthier – choices today.

Two years ago, I started exercising regularly with a friend of mine. She and I are pretty close to complete opposites – I've struggled with being overweight my whole life, while she waged a serious battle with anorexia in college. I wore XXL-size sweats for our workouts, and she shopped in the kiddie section to find clothes small enough to fit. But we were both on a journey toward health, and we started from where we were. (If you have a similar battle to mine, I pray that you have or find a friend like mine. Making the trip with someone who can encourage you not from the sidelines, but from right next to you, makes a huge difference.)

As we walked the treadmill, lifted weights, or rode bikes in the park, we talked about the things we wanted to accomplish in the arena of health. We set goals, some of them achievable within weeks or months, and others that were much more long-range. I could tell you a hundred stories from the experience, but I'll settle for telling you this: last October, we both rode the Jack and Back, a two-day 150km bike ride through the hills of Middle Tennessee. That was just the warm up for the 100+ miles of real hills in Tuscany, Italy that we conquered a few weeks later on a four-day biking trip. At the beginning of 2004, we started training for a sprint triathalon in June. That means I'm actually running voluntarily – without anyone chasing me. There truly is a first time for everything!

You'd never know by looking at me that I've accomplished such physical feats. I've still got more than a hundred pounds to lose. I'll certainly be in what they graciously call the "Athena" category at the triathalon (women over 150 lbs). But I don't care. I'll be running my Athena-sized rear end across the finish line of a race that a couple of years ago was not even imaginable for me. It wasn't an easy road. I made lots of starts and stops and wrong turns, and sometimes I went backwards for a little while and had to retrace my steps once I got turned around in the right direction again. I didn't get there overnight, and I didn't get there alone. But I got there.

Whatever your reason for picking up this book, I celebrate you for picking it up. Change your life. Start from wherever you are. Walk with the wise for health and vitality, starting today. I'll see you somewhere along the road!

Cheri Hoffman is a editor, writer, and photographer based in Nashville, Tennessee. You can contact her at 615.533.3388
or cheri@mentorsmagazine.com

www.mentorsmagazine.com

WALKING with the WISE
for Health & Vitality
Contributors

Alejandra Armas

Dr. Richard Baxter

Tom Bay, Ph.D.

Elsie Belcheff

Kevin E. Brown

Hyla Cass, M.D.

Deepak Chopra, M.D.

JC Colvin

Sam Defais

Brian K. Dennis, DDS

Linda Forsythe

Ann Louise Gittleman, Ph.D., C.N.S.

Judy Kay Gray, M.S.

Mark Victor Hansen

Cheri Hoffman

Dr. Cass Ingram

Dr. Marilyn Joyce, R.D.

Brad J. King, M.S., MFS

Dr. Marcus Laux

Joe Loiacano

Dr. Phil McGraw

Dr. Donald M. McLeod

Kim Muslusky

Lena Osborn

Shawn Phillips

Steven Rosenblatt, M.D., Ph.D.

Dr. Alan Rousso

Michael A. Schmidt, Ph.D.

Dr. Rick Swartzburg, D.C.

Marc St-Onge, BSc

Josef Tyls, MSc, Ph.D., Ind. Eng

Lorna R. Vanderhaeghe

Julian Whitaker, M.D.

Dr. Philip A. White

Nordine G. Zouareg

Are
YOU
A Mentor?

We are conducting a search for individuals with

the following qualities:

- Embody principles of integrity in life and business

- Possess expertise in a particular field with proficiency

  as a mentor, trainer, consultant or coach

- Possess unique information, inspiration or motivation

- Live according to the principles of true prosperity

- Have a passion to help and guide others

If you qualify, you may be eligible to become part of our team.
We publish articles and books, host mentorsmagazine.com,
sponsor live seminars, workshops,
teleseminars, and more!

Contact Us!

www.mentorsmagazine.com

MENTORS Publishing House, Inc.
10755-F Scripps Poway Pkwy. #530
San Diego, CA 92131

858-277-9700

INVEST IN
YOUR SUCCESS...

Tapes, Books, Boot Camps, Seminars, Newsletters and Coaching from our *WALKING* WITH THE *WISE* contributors are available at

www.mentorsmagazine.com

Move Forward with Boldness
on Your Quest
and Mighty Forces
Will Come to Your Aid

© 2004 Kim Muslusky

MENTORS *magazine motto*

Notes